# Profitable and Inclusive LinkedIn® Mastery

*Your Roadmap to Unlocking Brand Presence, Networking, and Financial Success for Professionals and Business Owners*

Samantha Lubanzu

Copyright © 2024 Samantha Lubanzu

**Profitable and Inclusive LinkedIn Mastery:** Your Roadmap to Unlocking Brand Presence, Networking, and Financial Success for Professionals and Business Owners

Written by Samantha Lubanzu

Published by Samantha Lubanzu Coaching Ltd ©

https://samanthalubanzu.com

This book and its content are Samantha Lubanzu Coaching Ltd © 2021 copyright. All rights reserved.

Any redistribution or reproduction of part or all of the contents in any form is prohibited other than the following:

You may not distribute or commercially exploit the content except with our express written permission. Nor may you transmit it or store it on any other website or other forms of electronic retrieval system or share it with third parties. This book and its content are copyrights of Samantha-Lubanzu-Coaching.

Samantha Ltd of electronic retrieval system or share with third parties -Ltd© Copyright.

This book is in no way authorised by, endorsed by, or affiliated with LinkedIn or its subsidiaries. All references to LinkedIn and other trademarked properties are used in accordance with the Fair Use Doctrine and are not meant to imply that this book is a LinkedIn product for advertising or other commercial purposes.

If you have any questions relating to this publication or the author, Samantha Lubanzu, please contact:

Website: samanthalubanzu.com

Email: Samantha@samanthalubanzu.com

## Table of Content

Table of Content
About the Author
Introduction
    Introduction Summary: Navigating the LinkedIn Landscape
Chapter One
LinkedIn Domination: Unveiling Your Niche for Explosive Growth
    Embarking on the LinkedIn Odyssey
    Decoding the Secrets of LinkedIn's Evolution
    Niche Unveiled: A Blueprint for Explosive Growth
    Niche Transformation Case Study: From Exploration to Domination
Chapter Two
Profile Powerhouse: Crafting an Inclusive LinkedIn Presence for Success
    Constructing Your Inclusive LinkedIn Identity
    The Foundation
        Your Profile Picture
        Your Professional Headline
        Pronouns
        Pronunciation
        Your Profile Banner
        The Summary /About Section
        Featured Section
        Skills and Endorsements
        Recommendations
        Volunteer Experience
        Publications
    Bringing It All Together
    Profile Makeover Case Study: Elevating Presence through Inclusivity
    Key Takeaways for Your LinkedIn Makeover
Chapter Three
Content Mastery: M.A.P.P.I.N.G. Your Inclusive Journey to LinkedIn Success
    Inclusive Content Mapping Case Study: A Journey to Viral Success
Chapter Four
Creator Catalyst: Unleashing Profit and Inclusion on LinkedIn
    Creator Spotlight: Realising Profit and Inclusion
Chapter Five

Content Alchemy: Unlocking Profitability and Inclusion on LinkedIn
    Transforming Content into Profitable Alchemy
    Planning Your Content
    Alchemy Success Stories: A Blend of Profit and Inclusion

Chapter Six
Engagement Elevator: Maximising Your LinkedIn Post Impact
    Elevated Engagement Case Study: From Likes to Leads
    The Impact of Strategic Profile Optimisation

Chapter Seven
Algorithm Decoded: Demystifying LinkedIn for Optimal Reach
    Deciphering the LinkedIn Algorithm
    Embracing the Algorithm

Chapter Eight
Link Power: Effectively Promoting External Links on LinkedIn
    Strategic Link Promotion: Unlocking External Link Power
        Understanding LinkedIn's Attitude Towards External Links

Chapter Nine
Leveraging Hashtags for Maximum LinkedIn Reach
    Understanding the Role of Hashtags
        Developing a Hashtag Strategy

Chapter Ten
Storytelling Mastery: Captivating Your LinkedIn Audience
    Mastering the Art of LinkedIn Storytelling

Chapter Eleven
Mastering LinkedIn's Artful Language for Success
    Crafting Copy that Converts

Chapter Twelve
Post Precision: Unlocking the Science Behind LinkedIn's Top Hits
    Precision in Post Creation
    Elements of A Viral LinkedIn Post
    Top Hit Stories: Crafting Viral Success

Bonus
    Roadmap to Follow
    Crafting a Strategic Content Plan

## About the Author

Samantha Lubanzu (She/Her) is a multi-award-winning diversity and inclusion strategist and advocate, a seasoned business and career coach, and distinguished alumni of the first UK LinkedIn Accelerator Programme. Her LinkedIn account has been under the *Invite Only* LinkedIn creator management program since 2022, hosted by LinkedIn themselves and her cool LinkedIn manager Ash. Her journey has been dedicated to helping thousands advance in their careers and businesses whilst leveraging LinkedIn to stand out in their brand presence, drive profitability, master effective networking and create a pipeline of lead generations.

As a sought-after speaker, consultant, author and thought leader, Samantha has significantly impacted the professional world. Her unique approach combines practical LinkedIn strategies with a deep commitment to building a more diverse, inclusive and prosperous professional landscape.

Samantha's relentless dedication to advancing diversity, inclusion, and professional success while helping individuals and organisations thrive on LinkedIn is evident on every page of the Profitable and Inclusive LinkedIn Mastery book.

Her passion for bridging the gap between profitability, inclusivity, effective networking, brand presence and genuine connections makes this book an invaluable resource for business owners and professionals eager to lead in a changing world.

Here are some reviews from Samantha's Profitable and Inclusive LinkedIn course from which this book is derived:

*"Do your business a favour, and book now! I'm so fortunate and grateful that I got a chance to work with Samantha at the very start of my business. Her expertise and recommendations have been invaluable to my strategy and to me personally. Many thanks for helping me craft a solid foundation that I can continue to build upon with confidence"* **~Allison Martinez, CEO**

*"This is a brilliant course to go on. An opportunity not to be missed. I learnt so much and had so much support. I was taught to go beyond my usual expectations by experiencing and developing the possibility of a better financial future. So enjoy your journey and good luck everyone"* **~M. Henry, CEO**

*"Sam's knowledge on LinkedIn is phenomenal! Sam's LinkedIn Mastery course was so informative with so much value shared. If you are looking to improve your understanding and leverage of*

LinkedIn, I would highly recommend attending Sam's course. Off to implement it all now. Thank you so much, Sam "**~Pam Molyneux, CEO**

## Introduction

Have you often thought that LinkedIn is just a noisy marketplace where everyone shouts and no one listens?

You're not alone.

So many users fail to see the true potential of the platform and end up wasting opportunities that would have yielded powerful relationships.

Picture this: endless posts, a sea of faces, all vying for attention – and there you are, wondering how to make your voice heard without selling your soul.

It's like trying to be heard at a rock concert, right?

You're striving to connect, to grow your business, to be inclusive, and, let's be real, to turn a profit.

But how do you cut through that noise with authenticity?

LinkedIn is one of the only platforms people go to with the explicit intention of doing business or networking, and it works best during office hours. It differs from other platforms where you can get lost with reels of a grand dinner or cats singing.

LinkedIn is different and intentional, making it the right place with many opportunities.

Here's the kicker: According to a report by IPSOS, 80% of B2B leads come from LinkedIn, yet only a fraction of content truly resonates. Also, the LinkedIn Audience 360 study reported that LinkedIn leads have a higher purchasing power and double as decision-makers at home, making it a goldmine for B2Cs to leverage attention using the right content strategy.

The truth is many business owners and professionals are being left behind.

Why?

Because most miss the mark on what matters - genuine, inclusive engagement.

You're probably thinking, 'Sure, but how do I do that without being just another face in the crowd?'

That's the million-dollar question, and guess what? You're about to find the answer.

This book isn't just a guide; it's your roadmap to mastering LinkedIn in a way that feels right to you. It's about making real connections, driving real business, and doing so in a way that values diversity and inclusion while making you profitable!

Whether you're an HR consultant, virtual assistant, business strategist, or any other professional, this book is tailored to enhance your expertise from novice to pro in record time.

How?

By tapping into the power of authenticity and understanding the fine distinction of this digital platform.

You will delve into my Profitable and Inclusive LinkedIn strategy and we'll see how my LinkedIn **MAPPING** formula ensures you win on LinkedIn.

In recent years, LinkedIn has evolved into a powerhouse of professional networking and business growth.

With over 830 million members worldwide as of 2023 and 40% of users reporting they use LinkedIn daily, the platform offers an unparalleled opportunity for you as professionals and business owners to expand your reach, build meaningful connections, and grow your businesses.

However, simply being on LinkedIn is not enough. To truly stand out, one must navigate the intricate dance of creating an impactful and inclusive presence.

It's no longer just about connecting with people; it's about engaging with them in a way that values diversity and fosters a sense of belonging.

A survey by LinkedIn itself showed that profiles with diverse and inclusive content have a 20% higher engagement rate, underlining the importance of an inclusive approach.

A report by McKinsey in 2023 also revealed that inclusive companies in the top quartile of board gender diversity are 27% more likely to outperform their competitors in the bottom quartile.

This book aims to guide you through leveraging this powerful combination of profitability and inclusivity.

As the digital era has made our world smaller but also more diverse. Your LinkedIn profile and content are not just seen by your immediate network but by a global audience. This book will teach you how to communicate effectively through social selling to a diverse audience.

You'll learn the intricacies of crafting a LinkedIn profile that speaks to a wide array of audiences, developing content strategies that not only engage but also respect and celebrate diversity while navigating LinkedIn's algorithms to maximise your reach.

These are strategies that will stand the test of time, even on an ever-evolving LinkedIn backdrop. We're going to dive deep into creating a presence that's not just profitable but profoundly inclusive. So, buckle up, let's begin this journey together, and transform your LinkedIn experience from overwhelming to outstanding."

## Introduction Summary: Navigating the LinkedIn Landscape

Step into the world of LinkedIn with Samantha Lubanzu, your guide in this transformative journey. As a multi-award-winning diversity and inclusion strategist and distinguished UK LinkedIn accelerator program Alumni, Samantha unravels the intricate layers of LinkedIn, turning it from a platform into a dynamic force for professional and business success. This is not just a guide; it's a manifesto for those seeking to elevate LinkedIn into a catalyst for success. The journey spans from understanding LinkedIn's evolution to crafting compelling profiles, decoding algorithms, mastering storytelling, and unveiling real-life success stories.

**Description:** Introduction to LinkedIn's transformative potential and its role in reshaping careers, businesses, and inclusivity. Highlights the importance of LinkedIn as a tool for effective networking.

# Chapter One

# LinkedIn Domination: Unveiling Your Niche for Explosive Growth

You have taken a bold step by deciding to be intentional with your LinkedIn profile, and together, we'll turn your LinkedIn game on its head! This chapter is about making LinkedIn a powerhouse for your unique brand.

Here, we're not just skimming the surface but diving deep. We will unwrap the layers of LinkedIn, getting to the heart of what makes this platform a goldmine for those who know how to use it.

It involves finding your spot, your voice, and your community.

It's where your unique blend of talents, experiences, and passions meet an audience that's been waiting just for you.

In this chapter, we'll journey through the twists and turns of LinkedIn's story, understanding how its past shapes our present opportunities.

We're going to learn from real stories, real triumphs - and yep, that includes my journey, too. These aren't just feel-good stories; they're the meat and potatoes, the real deal of what it takes to carve out your niche and own it.

## Embarking on the LinkedIn Odyssey

Can you remember the first time you logged into LinkedIn? Maybe you felt a bit lost, like stepping into a bustling city where everyone seemed to know their way except you.

That's how I felt, too.

Fresh out of university, eager yet clueless, I saw LinkedIn as nothing more than a digital CV holder. But just like any journey, the real magic of LinkedIn unfolds when you start exploring its unique features.

Imagine LinkedIn as a vast, unfamiliar digital continent, a rich and diverse landscape that pulses with the potential for growth and success. It's a place where every turn and every connection opens up new paths and possibilities.

Just like when you stand at the ocean's edge, feeling its vastness, LinkedIn stretches out in front of you, filled with opportunities waiting just beneath the surface.

This digital continent is not just a network; it's a thriving community of professionals, dreamers, doers, and thinkers - all linked together.

Every profile, every post is a story, a journey, and a chance to learn and grow. It's where ambition meets opportunity, your unique skills can find their spotlight, and your voice can echo in the corridors of industries and niches far and wide.

But here's the catch: standing out is no small feat, just like in a crowded market. You've got to be more than just present; you need to shine to catch the eye amid the hustle and bustle.

That's where the journey begins—finding that unique spark, your niche, that sets you apart in the pool of talent and ambition.

With LinkedIn, any new connection you make is an opportunity for potential collaboration, every group a forum of ideas, and every job post a doorway to new beginnings.

LinkedIn helps you discover many opportunities - from networking that connects you with like-minded professionals to brand building that lets your personal brand shine.

But it's more than just connecting; it's about building long-lasting relationships. You get to share your journey and insights while learning from the wealth of diverse experiences surrounding you.

And let's not forget the power of thought leadership - sharing your wisdom, sparking conversations, and influencing change.

You should approach LinkedIn not just as a user but as an explorer and a pioneer in your own right. Whether you are a seasoned professional, business owner, or just starting out, LinkedIn is a landscape that rewards those who approach it with intention, curiosity, and a readiness to engage and grow.

Stick with me as we dive deeper to see how you can find and fully explore your niche.

## Decoding the Secrets of LinkedIn's Evolution

Over time, LinkedIn has evolved as the dynamics of human nature continue to change. It has become a platform where conventional methods are challenged, and platform users explore other means of business growth.

Let's take a moment to journey back to how it all started.

LinkedIn began as a simple idea in 2003: a space for professionals to connect, grow, and flourish. They had their profiles set up, and it served as a directory.

By 2006, it wasn't just a directory; it was a place to find jobs or to hunt for that next big opportunity.

Fast forward to 2012, LinkedIn wasn't just growing; it was blossoming, introducing features like endorsements and making the platform not just about connecting but also about nurturing and validating professional skills.

With each milestone, LinkedIn continued to stretch its boundaries.

It became more than just a network; it became a global professional hub where over 700 million people converge to share, learn, and inspire.

And this is why you need to take advantage of this to build your brand and business.

LinkedIn's transformation reflects a shift in how we approach careers and professional branding. It's no longer just about who you know; it's about who knows you and what you stand for.

LinkedIn's growth has been like a stone thrown into the professional pond, creating waves that have touched every corner of the job market and business world.

The way we network has transformed; it now goes beyond the conventional exchange of business cards at conferences. You can now build meaningful connections, engage with content, and share insights.

## Niche Unveiled: A Blueprint for Explosive Growth

Carving out your niche on LinkedIn involves claiming your domain, where you're not just another face in the crowd. You need to stand out and truly connect with your diverse audience.

But how do you go about it?

It's simpler and yet more profound than you might think.

To begin, peel back the layers to discover what you're genuinely passionate about. This isn't about jumping on the latest trend or mirroring someone else's success path.

It's about digging deep and asking yourself, "What lights my fire? What can I talk about for hours without losing steam?"

Your niche should intersect your expertise, your passions, and the market's needs. It's where you can add real value, where your insights and experiences can make a difference.

Think about it. When you try to appeal to the masses, your message gets diluted. But when you zero in on a particular area, your voice becomes louder and clearer.

It's counterintuitive, right?

You'd think casting a wider net would yield more results, but the magic happens when you narrow your focus.

Do not try to be all things to all people. You must create an ideal client avatar to know exactly whom you serve.

Here are the steps to create your avatar to ensure you think of a diverse perspective.

Do your research and identify your ideal clients' pain points.

To find the pain points of your ideal client:

- Look on "Ask the Public"
- Check comments to see the conversation going on
- Go into groups and view their conversation on there
- Attend events and lives

When communicating with your ideal audience, use their language, not your own.

Next, it's crucial to validate this niche. This means doing a bit of homework to ensure there's an appetite for what you're offering.

LinkedIn is a treasure trove of data and insights. Use it!

Look at what conversations are happening in your proposed niche

Are there questions being asked that you can answer? Are there gaps in the knowledge that you can fill? This is where you start to see the blueprint for your explosive growth taking shape.

Once you've honed in on your niche, it's about embodying it in every aspect of your LinkedIn presence. Your profile should scream your niche from the rooftop.

Each of your offers should also have a different ideal client persona. Here is an example of how I have structured my offers based on their personas:

- **The Career Accelerator CPD certified Programme**
    - Ambitious women of colour and allies.
    - Who want to accelerate their careers and businesses to the highest level so they can emerge into their true purpose as the successful, confident, and highly valued women that they were designed to be and still enjoy a balanced home and work life.
- **Profitable And Inclusive LinkedIn Mastery**
    - For professionals or Business owners looking to build their LinkedIn knowledge with the right inclusive content strategy.
- **90 minutes Profitable & inclusive LinkedIn Intensive programme or Done For You LinkedIn Content Strategy**
    - For professionals or business owners looking to scale their businesses on LinkedIn with the right inclusive content strategy.
    - They want to accelerate their careers and businesses to the highest level.
- **Diversity & Inclusion Evolve CPD certified programme**
    - For HR/ business Leaders or Business owners who would like to operate a more diverse and inclusive business.

From your headline to your summary, your posts to your comments, everything should align with the niche you claim, especially as a diverse and inclusive business champion.

This consistency builds your brand, turning your LinkedIn profile into a beacon for those seeking knowledge and insight in your area.

But then again, finding your niche is not a one-and-done deal. It's an ongoing journey of refinement and evolution. As the market changes, as your business grows, your niche may shift, and that's perfectly okay.

The key is to stay authentic, stay engaged, and keep your finger on the pulse of your audience's needs, ensuring inclusivity in every strand. Starting out may seem challenging, but as you keep at it, you'll build a solid presence.

When I started using LinkedIn, I had no specific niche or direction for my content. But here's the thing: the moment I began to treat LinkedIn not as a digital dump but as a vibrant community to engage with, things started to change.

And it all began with finding my niche.

At first, I was a generalist, trying to appeal to everyone and ending up connecting with no one. Only when I honed in on HR, sharing my journey, insights, and the ups and downs of climbing the career ladder, I started to see real engagement.

Let's not forget that identifying your niche and making it your own on LinkedIn opens up a world of opportunities and establishes you as the go-to expert in your field.

Identifying your niche on LinkedIn does not limit you. Rather, it helps you find your tribe: those who get you need your insights and are looking for exactly what you have to offer.

For me, it was the HR community focused on diversity and inclusion. By focusing on HR, I started attracting the right kind of attention from recruiters and began to establish myself as someone to watch in the field.

I started sharing my successes and lessons I learned along the way. I talked about the challenges of transitioning from a university student to an HR professional, the power of voluntary roles in gaining real-world experience, and the importance of being visible and proactive on LinkedIn.

It was authentic, it was real, and it resonated.

As a mother of six under six children who, despite struggling and waiting for years to conceive, still runs a successful business.

My IVF journey was not an easy one, and I also had a set of premature twins, but I still kept building my career and growing. I have felt vulnerable sharing the story of my personal struggles.

What I have gone through has become a part of my growth, and telling this story makes people see the real me. My authenticity shines through and strengthens my niche as a diversity and inclusion coach for women (and Allies).

Being an inclusive and diverse business champion, your niche guides your content, shapes your interactions, and determines the trajectory of your journey on the platform.

By unveiling and embracing your niche, you're not just growing your LinkedIn presence but setting the stage for explosive growth in your business and beyond. It's a bold move that pays dividends in visibility, influence, and impact. So, take the plunge, find your niche, and watch as the doors to new opportunities swing wide open.

## Niche Transformation Case Study: From Exploration to Domination

Let me share my experience, a journey that started with a simple login.

Imagine a uni student, eager yet utterly baffled by the digital landscape of LinkedIn. That was me, standing on the brink of the professional world, armed with nothing but ambition and a CV that echoed my confusion.

LinkedIn seemed like a maze with no clear entry point. I'd hop on, tweak a few things, and hop off, convinced it was nothing more than a digital billboard for my CV.

Fast forward, and there I was, dipping my toes into the HR pool. It hit me like a ton of bricks - LinkedIn wasn't just a static display but dynamic, pulsating with potential connections and opportunities.

It dawned on me that this platform could be my stage, a place to broadcast my growing expertise and passions within HR.

I started small, updating my profile to mirror my shift into HR, sharing snippets of my journey as the CIPD Ambassador lead, and whispering into the LinkedIn void that I was on the lookout for HR roles.

To my surprise, the void whispered back. emails and DMs from recruiters began trickling in, turning my once barren LinkedIn inbox into a treasure trove of opportunities.

But the real game-changer was when I decided to not just exist on LinkedIn but truly dominate it.

I began sharing more than just updates; I shared stories, insights, the highs and lows of my journey. I was no longer just looking for opportunities; I was creating them.

My profile transformed from a mere CV to a beacon for headhunters seeking HR professionals. I'd unwittingly stumbled upon my niche and by doing so, unlocked a new realm of possibilities.

It wasn't just about being visible; it was about being vividly present, engaging in a way that drew people in, made them linger, and ultimately, connect- it was also being vulnerable (some of my stories cut like a knife to share, but I felt free when I shared and it resonated with my ideal audience perfectly).

As I took the plunge and left the corporate world, I wanted to help women, especially women of colour, navigate the career ladder and land their dream roles.

I honed this craft further with the help of a LinkedIn coach, who steered me towards writing with purpose - focusing on hooks, stories, value, and a call to action. This wasn't just posting; this was strategic storytelling.

And although I had a coach, something steered me to make my own mark, to be a little different.

I started the painful but necessary journey of sharing my experiences of racism, sexism, bullying, and microaggressions in the workplace.

Although my story was hard, I knew it was not unique, and as I shared, it resonated! I started to get an influx of DMs sharing their own personal stories similar to mine, corporations wanting support to create strategies in the workplace, and invites to speak on stages.

The impact? Monumental.

My LinkedIn profile became a magnet for job offers, speaking engagements, workshop requests, and coaching opportunities. I was approached by well-known tech companies, charities, household names, and individuals wanting to make their own stamp on the world.

And then I was approached directly by LinkedIn...It was unbelievable!

I got an invite-only opportunity to be in their LinkedIn creator management programme. I was scheduled to work with my LinkedIn manager Ash, who invited me into a new world of behind-the-scenes that very few have the privilege of being invited into, yet I was invited!

One of the insights behind the LinkedIn scenes was the opportunity to test new beta products and be the first to know when updates were released and what new features would be added. I also got opportunities to be featured on LinkedIn news (one of my posts went viral, with mine sitting next to Richard Branson's).

**Post analytics**

Samantha Lubanzu MCIPD 🧑 Career/ Biz Coach for Women ...
MY SUPERPOWERS REVEALED 🧑
I know you have been... see more

**Discovery** ❓

**138,758**
Impressions

It was as if I had cracked a secret code, unlocking a level of engagement and connection I hadn't thought possible.

LinkedIn had morphed from a daunting digital landscape into a fertile ground for growth and opportunities.

I went from simply seeking job opportunities to being known for coaching women, especially women of colour looking to move into senior roles.

I also became known for using my HR knowledge to create impactful, action-oriented, results-driven diversity and inclusion strategies for corporates and small business owners.

I was featured in numerous publications, including high-profile Conde Nasté Glamour to HR Management and HR Director magazine. I won awards and became known as one of the top Diversity and Inclusion coaches in Manchester, UK.

In the meantime, I was also successfully selected in the prestigious LinkedIn first UK Accelerator programme for my SuperWomenCan Podcast idea to tell more stories of success and resilience for women of colour!, which I went on to launch with LinkedIn.

This journey from exploration to domination on LinkedIn underscores a powerful truth:

Finding and owning your niche isn't just about standing out; it's about standing true to what makes you, you, and sharing not just what you do but who you are, and by doing so, attracting the very opportunities that resonate with your authentic self.

I transformed my LinkedIn presence through consistent engagement, authentic storytelling, and strategic visibility. It became a testament to the power of finding one's niche and leveraging it to advance one's career. One where you inspire, connect and lead within the digital professional community.

This story isn't just mine; it's a blueprint for anyone willing to dive deep, discover their niche, and dominate it on LinkedIn. It's a call to move beyond the superficial and share your journey, insights, and authentic self. Because in the end, that's what truly resonates, what truly connects, and what ultimately transforms.

Next step: Get the worksheet below to help you unveil your niche and begin your LinkedIn transformation.

Scan here for a downloadable worksheet from the resource page:

**The Niche Unveiled Action Pack**

## Chapter Two

## Profile Powerhouse: Crafting an Inclusive LinkedIn Presence for Success

Building a LinkedIn profile that mirrors your profession or business while embracing inclusivity isn't just about ticking boxes or stuffing keywords.

It involves weaving a narrative so compelling, so authentic that it draws people in, inviting them to see the world through your lens, to appreciate the rich experiences that make you who you are whilst appreciating the differences and needs of your diverse ideal audience, too.

Think of your LinkedIn as the front porch of your professional home. What do you want passersby to see? More importantly, what do you want them to feel as they pause and peer in? You want a profile that says, "Here lives a professional who not only respects but champions diversity." And isn't that a breath of fresh air in the often stale, monochrome world of professional networking?

The truth is the more personal and connected your profile feels, the more professional it actually becomes. It turns out those little personal touches don't make you or your business less professional—they make you more approachable, more relatable, and, yes, more respected.

So, how can you shift from a generic billboard to a dynamic, inclusive showcase of your professional journey? Here's how you can blend your values with your career achievements to create a LinkedIn profile that tells and truly speaks.

### Constructing Your Inclusive LinkedIn Identity

Ready to do the work that will make your profile stand out? Here are the elements to focus on for creating an inclusive LinkedIn presence:

### The Foundation

The best way to begin your LinkedIn transformation is to start with the basics, but think of them as anything but basic. Your profile picture and headline aren't just placeholders; they're your first hello, your digital handshake.

**Your Profile Picture**

This first impression often hinges on your profile picture in the professional world, especially on LinkedIn.

It's your digital handshake, your visual business card.

**Amanda Hutchinson, owner and brand photographer at AKP Branding Stories,** states that "research has shown that people form a first impression in just 50 milliseconds, a fraction of a second! Therefore, it is crucial to make a solid first impression, and this is where high-quality, consistent and professional brand photography comes into play."

She also adds that "articles with relevant images get 94% more views on average compared to articles with no images. And having a professional image makes the content, including your profile, more memorable, with recall increasing from 10% with text-only content to 65% for content with a photo after 3 days."

Scan Here to Follow Amanda on Linkedin.

Using high-quality, professional images in your profile photo, banner, and posts is more than just vanity; it's a commitment to your personal brand.

**So, be sure to pop your profile picture on visible.**

Here's how to do it ...

First, click the blue plus sign on your profile photo and tap View/Edit profile at the bottom.

Select the "Public" visibility option for your profile.

The change is saved automatically.

LinkedIn profiles with professional images come across as credible and trustworthy. But here's an interesting twist that only celebrities know – research suggests that showing your hands, holding a coffee cup, or simply resting in view amplifies perceptions of trustworthiness and openness.

It's like your photo says, "Here I am, open and ready to connect!"

Imagine this: Would you feel confident purchasing a car from a salesperson with their hands behind their back?

Or even a burger from a chef who won't let you see the grill - something's definitely sizzling, but it might not be what you ordered!

Like other platforms, LinkedIn loves content that pops with clear, professional imagery and conveys trust.

Why?

Because it grabs attention and halts the mindless scrolling.

Now, you might wonder, "What if I can't have a professional shoot?" No worries, you can still create a stellar image.

So, what makes a professional-looking image if you can't have a professional shoot?

First up, lighting – it's the secret sauce of photography. Natural light works wonders, so position yourself near a window or an open door. But watch out for the midday sun; it can cast harsh, unflattering shadows.

Next, the backdrop. Keep it neat and unobtrusive. Remember, you're the star of this show; the background is just the stage.

Lastly, your attire. Dress in a way that reflects your personal brand and the image you want to project. Think about who'll be scrolling through LinkedIn and stumbling upon your profile. This isn't the time for your flashy party attire unless, of course, that's your industry – then, by all means, let your style shine!

In essence, your LinkedIn photo is a powerful tool in your professional toolkit. It's not just a picture; it's a portrayal of your professionalism, credibility, and approachability.

Choose a photo where your confidence and warmth shine through, one that says, "Hey, I'm glad you're here."

Here's an example of a good profile picture:

Samantha Lubanzu          Steven Bartlett

The importance of a good professional photo cannot be overemphasised. Make sure to include a professional-looking profile photo and a company logo to stand out.

**Your Professional Headline**

Next up is your headline. You need to craft a headline that's not just a job title but a headline that tells a story.

Your headline is your stage. This is where you tell your story, listing achievements and sharing your journey. How did you get here? What challenges did you overcome? What drives you? This is your chance to showcase your inclusivity journey and show your business and profile's inclusive and diverse side.

When you share from the heart, you create a space for others to see themselves in your story, to feel included and inspired.

Maybe you championed diversity initiatives or are passionate about mentoring underrepresented talents. Whatever it is, let your passion and purpose shine through.

But here's the kicker – it's not enough to say it; you need to show it.

Use specific examples. Did you lead a campaign that broke down barriers? Tell us about it.

Did you mentor someone and watch them soar? Share that story.

Your headline needs to outline what you do, why you do it and what sets you apart from your competitors.

Are you an "HR Professional"?

How about

"**Empowering HR Innovation | Building Inclusive Cultures**"?

Or

Instead of "Marketing Manager," you could say:

"**Strategising Brand Architect | Crafting Compelling Marketing Narratives for Impactful Engagement.**"

Or

Rather than "Software Engineer," try:

"**Tech Trailblazer | Pioneering Software Solutions for a Connected World.**"

Or

Instead of "Financial Analyst," consider

"**Numbers Whisperer | Guiding Financial Success through Analytical Insight.**"

These headlines not only describe the role but also highlight the impact and passion behind it.

See the difference?

You're not just sharing what you do; you're sharing how you make a difference.

Ensure that your profile is up-to-date and professional. LinkedIn profiles should be kept current with accurate information that reflects the most recent activities of your business.

Ensure that you add relevant keywords you want to be associated with so that you can be found when people search for those keywords.

Here are the steps for creating your headline:

To edit your professional headline:

1. Click the 🔘 **Me** icon at top of your LinkedIn homepage.

2. Click **View Profile**.

3. Click the ✏️ **Edit** icon in your introduction section.

4. In the **Edit intro** pop-up window, make your changes in the **Headline** field.

5. Click **Save**.

**Source:** LinkedIn.com

If you opt for LinkedIn Premium, you can access an AI-powered feature that helps craft your profile headline. If you choose to utilise this tool, take the time to refine it in your profile to make it more compelling and effective.

Example of my LinkedIn profile headline:

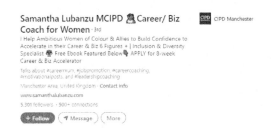

Here, I have my name as part of my headline.

So, my name is not actually my title. It's just my name. And yes, I put it this way. But there's a downside to me having my name in my title, which also says "**Career/Biz Coach For Women**". Although it stands out and lets people know what you do, when it comes to verification, which is a new feature on LinkedIn, it won't allow you to be verified unless you've got your correct name.

I would recommend that you make a decision when writing your headline. If you want to have the blue verification tick on your profile, then you need to have just your name. But if you prefer to stand out, then you can add other attributes.

Having the blue verification tick obviously comes with the security of people knowing that you are real, and I have been able to still verify myself in the background with my books. However, I will not be given the blue tick unless I update my name.

Here's how to get verified on LinkedIn, note that the verification process is free of charge:

**Step 1: Start the Verification Process**

- Navigate to your LinkedIn profile.
- Click on the "More" button, usually found next to your profile section.
- From the dropdown menu, select "About this profile."

**Step 2: Initiate Identity Verification**

- Click on "Get verified" under the identity verification section.

- A QR code will appear. Use your mobile device to scan this code, which will redirect you to the CLEAR verification service.

**Step 3: Complete the CLEAR Verification Steps**

- Follow the instructions provided by CLEAR. This will include taking a photo of yourself and uploading a government-issued ID.
- Once prompted, select "Yes, share" to allow LinkedIn access to your verification information from CLEAR.

**Step 4: Confirmation of Verification**

- After submitting your information, LinkedIn will compare the name on your LinkedIn profile with the name on your government-issued ID.
- If the names match, LinkedIn will grant you a verification badge. This badge may also display the name of the issuing country of your ID.

**Step 5: Viewing Your Verification Badge**

- Once verified, a small grey badge will appear next to your name on your profile.
- You can click on this badge to view more information about the type and method of your verification.

This process is designed to be user-friendly and accessible, helping you enhance your credibility on the platform without any associated costs.

That's it, you're done!

**Next**, let your audience know if you have an article you want them to read or a feature or a freebie within the banner section, and invite them to get it using a call to action.

It's these snippets of realness that transform your profile from a CV to a canvas, painting a picture of a leader who not just talks the talk but walks the walk.

When creating your LinkedIn headline, don't forget to be inclusive. You can rephrase statements like "anyone can do it" to be more inclusive and respectful.

Instead, focus on the accessibility or simplicity of the task without implying that it's effortless for everyone.

For example:

**"Accessible for All: Achieve [Outcome] with Just a few Minutes a Day!"**

**"Designed for All Abilities: in just a Few Minutes Daily"**

This revision emphasises the accessibility of the task without suggesting that it's universally easy for everyone. It acknowledges that the activity can be completed by many people while respecting individual differences and abilities.

## Pronouns

On LinkedIn, you have the option to add pronouns like "she/her," "he/him," or "they/them" to your profile. Setting up this feature is a small but meaningful step toward inclusivity and respect for gender diversity.

It's an opportunity to ensure that others know how you prefer to be addressed and create a more inclusive environment for everyone. Let's walk through how to set up this feature on your LinkedIn profile.

Click on the pen close to your profile name.

Select pronouns, then save

## Pronunciation

It's quite a common experience to see people struggling with pronouncing my surname name, "Lubanzu." For me, it's the simplest word, but for those encountering it for the first time, a little helping hand goes a long way.

Luckily, LinkedIn offers a feature that allows you to add pronunciation, which is incredibly helpful. And it's not just about helping others; it's about inclusivity.

Even seemingly common names like "Emma" can be perceived differently across the globe. Taking the time to acknowledge and accommodate these differences is important.

Paying attention to how individuals perceive and pronounce your name and those on the platform is crucial, especially if they're considering working with you. It shows respect for their cultural background and demonstrates your commitment to inclusivity and understanding.

Plus, it sets a positive tone for your professional relationship right from the start. So, taking the time to ensure your name is pronounced correctly and likewise doing the same for others can make a significant difference in how others perceive you and your professionalism.

Adding this feature on LinkedIn is straightforward. Let me guide you through it.

As you did previously, click on the pen close to your name. Then, scroll down to pronunciation.

Click on "Add name pronunciation"

Press the big blue record button to record your name, then click "Save."

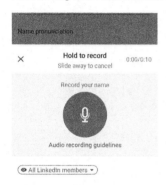

**Your Profile Banner**

A profile banner is like the shop window to your online presence. It's the first thing people see when they visit your profile, so it sets the tone and gives them a glimpse into who you are or what you're about.

Plus, it's a great way to make a memorable impression and stand out from the crowd in a visually appealing way.

So, having an eye-catching and relevant profile banner can help attract attention, convey your personality or brand, and make your profile more inviting and engaging to visitors.

Add a banner photo just above your profile picture, including who you are, what you do, and major achievements. Use your business logo, a professional photo of you, and, for extra credibility, any "Featured in" logos within the banner.

Adding a professional photo of yourself on your banner can help draw individuals in and foster connections. Additionally, showcasing any books or publications you've written can further enhance your profile and highlight your expertise and accomplishments.

It is also important to talk about your transformation statement in your banner.

Here is a quick idea template for your banner:

- I help... to...
- HR consultant by day ..... superhero CIPD volunteer by night
- Expert LinkedIn Strategist + Trainer. Business & Career Coach. DEI Speaker. FREE Training: "How I Made Multiple 6 Figures on LinkedIn"↓

And remember to have a call to action.

E.g. **Get my free quiz below:**

With the Premium option, you can now select and add "Book a call" or "Visit my store" with your links, and this is displayed clearly just beneath your profile whenever you leave a comment on posts.

Example of an engaging banner:

You can see above that I highlight myself holding my Diversity and Inclusion Unlocked book in the picture to show credibility.

## The Summary /About Section

The About section of your LinkedIn profile is your professional narrative's heart. It's where you craft a compelling story that not just outlines your achievements but also brings your personality and passions to the forefront. Here's how to make your About section resonate with authenticity, inclusivity, and engagement.

**Start with a Hook:** Begin your About section with a captivating opener that draws readers in. Consider starting with a question, a surprising fact, or a bold statement that reflects your professional ethos. For instance, "Have you ever wondered how inclusive leadership can transform a workplace?"

**Share Your Journey:** After grabbing attention, dive into your professional journey. Explain not just what you do, but why you do it. What motivated you to choose your career path? What challenges have you faced, and how have you overcome them? This isn't just about listing jobs—it's about showing the evolution of your passion and expertise.

**Highlight Your Impact:** Discuss specific projects or roles where you've made a significant impact. Use metrics and specific outcomes to demonstrate your contributions. For example, "Led a diversity initiative that increased company-wide cultural competency by 40% over two years."

**Inclusivity in Action:** Since inclusivity is a key theme, illustrate how you've championed diversity and inclusion in your roles. Maybe you've mentored underrepresented groups, or initiated policies that enhance accessibility. Show how these efforts align with your professional values.

**Connect on a Personal Level:** Make your summary personal and relatable. Share a bit about your interests outside of work or how your personal experiences have shaped your professional outlook. This humanises your profile and makes you more approachable.

**Call to Action:** End with an invitation or a call to action. Encourage visitors to connect with you, check out a project, or participate in a conversation. For example, "Let's connect and discuss how we can create more inclusive workplaces together."

**Professional Yet Approachable Tone:** Throughout your About section, maintain a professional yet approachable tone. Use clear, concise language that reflects your personality. This helps create a connection with the reader and makes your profile memorable.

Make sure to feature keywords that will help you get found in searches and optimise your profile for maximum visibility.

**Top Inclusion Tip:** Ensure you avoid ableist language. For example, avoid using phrases such as "anyone can do it!" instead say, "It can be done in only 5 minutes a day by anyone!".

Here is a business example "About" section:

> Hello !
> Are you looking to [Value Add] but not sure where to start?
> Look no further!
> I'm [Name], and my superpower is helping [Ideal Client].
> My program helps clients achieve their goals by tackling key topics such as:
> —[Topic/Module]
> —[Topic/Module]
> —[Topic/Module]
>
> —[Topic/Module]
>
> —{TOPIC}_MODULE]}
>
> With this framework, many of my clients have already discovered amazing results. Reviews like '[Testimonial]' from {CLIENT NAME & TITLE}, and others show how powerful the impact can be.
>
> Not only that, but I've put these methods into practice myself- achieving success in areas including press coverage,[Press, Business Metric Speaking Awards and MORE!.
>
> I'd love for us to connect on LinkedIn or via other links found on my profile so we can discuss your future dreams And ambitions - let's get them fulfilled today!

Here is a professional example "About" section:

Are you passionate about building workplaces where everyone feels valued and heard?

So am I. I'm [Your Name], a dedicated [Your Job Title] with over a decade of experience in fostering inclusive work environments.

From my early days as a [Previous Relevant Job Title], I learned the powerful impact of inclusive practices on employee engagement and innovation.

Driven by a passion to bring about positive change, I've spearheaded initiatives that have not only enhanced diversity but have also driven business outcomes. For instance, at [Company Name], I led a team that developed a diversity training program, resulting in a 40% increase in minority leadership roles within two years.

But my commitment goes beyond the boardroom. As a [Volunteer Position], I've worked with community leaders to support career development for young adults from underrepresented backgrounds. These experiences have deepened my understanding of how diverse perspectives are crucial for true innovation.

Outside the office, I'm an avid reader and occasional marathon runner, pursuits that teach me resilience and persistence—qualities I bring into my professional life.

Let's connect and push the boundaries of what we can achieve through inclusivity. Feel free to reach out to discuss potential collaborations or just to share ideas on creating a more inclusive world.

This approach to the About section weaves together your professional achievements and personal values, creating a narrative that invites connections and encourages engagement on both professional and personal levels.

**Featured Section**

Having a Featured section on your profile is a great way to highlight key experiences, accomplishments, and projects you're proud of. By featuring content in this section, it will be seen more often by potential employers, as well as other professionals who view your profile.

You can also add a short video about yourself, what you do, and how you help people. This gives people the opportunity to get to know you. The video should be concise and professional.

Note that LinkedIn no longer allows you to record and add a video to your banner. The workaround is to add it to the "Featured In" section.

You

Here is an example of my "Featured section" on LinkedIn

**Top tip:** My feature section changes depending on "My current" campaign. In this example, I am showcasing my clients' achievements of obtaining LinkedIn Top Voice and other LinkedIn client success stories. If you can include a link to a downloadable resource or programme, here is the perfect place.

**Skills and Endorsements**

Here's where you can really shine. Highlight skills that reflect your professional expertise and your commitment to inclusivity.

And don't just wait for endorsements. Be proactive.

Endorse your colleagues, especially those from underrepresented groups whose skills you genuinely admire.

It's a way of amplifying voices that might not always be heard.

**Recommendations**

This is gold. Seek recommendations from a diverse group of colleagues, mentors, and mentees. These testimonials give depth to your profile, offering multifaceted insights into who you are as a professional and a champion for inclusivity. It's one thing to claim you're committed to diversity; it's another when others attest to it.

Here's an example of my LinkedIn recommendations:

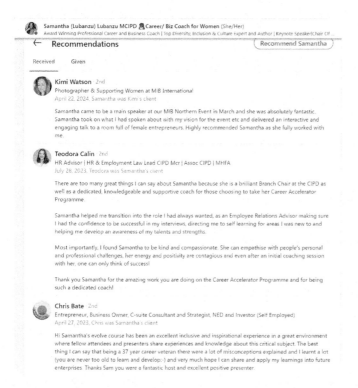

Note that recommendation is a two-way thing; just as you have received it, remember to give recommendations for others, too!

**Volunteer Experience**

Adding your volunteer experiences to your LinkedIn profile shows where you've invested your energy and how you've nurtured your community.

This section showcases your commitment to causes and initiatives beyond the boardroom, reflecting your personal values and your dedication to making a difference. Here's how to give your volunteer experiences the spotlight they deserve on LinkedIn.

First, think about the types of volunteering you've engaged in. Have you helped organise community clean-ups? Mentored young professionals? Served on the board of a nonprofit? Each of these experiences tells a story of the work done and the leadership and passion you bring to the table.

When listing your volunteer roles, start with the organisation's name and your role or title.

But don't stop there—describe your responsibilities and contributions. Did you lead a team? Did you initiate a new programme? How did your involvement bring about change or benefit the cause? Be specific about your impact.

For example:

**Nonprofit Organisation Name - Board Member**

**Duration:** January 2020 - Present

Spearheaded a campaign that raised £50,000 for literacy programmes, increasing the organisation's outreach by 20%.

Organised monthly workshops for community leaders, enhancing local engagement and fostering new partnerships.

Next, reflect on the skills you developed or used during your volunteer work. Leadership, project management, fundraising, and cross-cultural communication are just a few skills that volunteering can highlight. Connecting these skills to your professional narrative shows how your volunteer experiences enrich your capabilities.

Incorporate any recognition or achievements related to your volunteering. Were you acknowledged or awarded for your efforts? Highlighting these recognitions can add a layer of authenticity and accomplishment to your profile.

Finally, think about the broader implications of your volunteer work. How does it connect to your professional goals or personal mission? Make it clear that your professional life is intertwined with a commitment to giving back.

Here is an example from my profile on how to showcase your volunteer experience.

> **Volunteering** +
>
> **Call Center Representative**
> Pregnant Then Screwed
> Jan 2021 - Jun 2022 · 1 yr 6 mos
> Human Rights
>
> As an Expert HR Law Advisor Volunteer on The HR Advice Line, I provide crucial support to individuals facing workplace discrimination due to pregnancy, maternity leave, or parenthood. With 20+ years of experience, I offered guidance on flexible working requests, redundancy rights, maternity pay/leave, and legal protections against discrimination. I supported to navigate challenging situations, ensuring everyone's rights are upheld in the workplace.
>
> Examples of the powerful work we do:
>
> 1. A woman faced workplace discrimination due to pregnancy; we supported her through legal advice and mentorship, leading to a £185,000 settlement.
>
> 2. We're advocating for changes in laws to prevent maternity discrimination, while continuing to provide support to those in need.

## Publications

You can update your profile and add relevant publications to your niche. This adds a layer of credibility to your profile and also shows your dedication to the cause you champion.

Here's a list publication I have added to my profile:

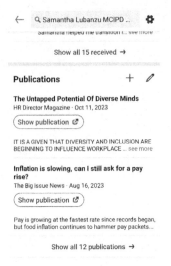

## Bringing It All Together

Crafting an inclusive LinkedIn presence goes beyond a well-written profile. You must create a living, breathing testament to your values, journey, and commitment to making the professional world a more inclusive space.

You need to show up, not just as a professional and business owner, but as a person deeply invested in building bridges, breaking down barriers, and bringing people together.

Remember, your LinkedIn profile isn't just a reflection of you; it's a beacon of what you stand for, and you should make it count.

## Profile Makeover Case Study: Elevating Presence through Inclusivity

Creating a LinkedIn profile needs to feel like you are telling a story. It should have a compelling narrative that draws your target audience from the first line.

So, what turns a good profile into a magnetic one?

It's the pulse of authenticity, the embrace of diversity, and a clear, welcoming beacon of inclusivity. You need to create a welcoming space that resonates with a diverse audience.

Let's look at the LinkedIn elements on my profile and how I positioned my profile for success. You can take a look at my profile here:

https://www.linkedin.com/in/samantha-lubanzu-career-business-coach/

Scan the QR code to view my profile:

### The Headline: More Than a Job Title

Forget the standard "Job Title at Company." My headline reads like a banner headline on the front page of your favourite newspaper. It's bold, brave, and makes you want to read on.

It says, "**Samantha Lubanzu MCIPD 🏆 Career/ Biz Coach for Women**"

In fewer than 120 characters, I've not just introduced myself; I've made a statement. It's clear I'm not here to play the game; I'm here to change it.

It also shows that I am qualified and have the right certifications:

Award Winning Professional Career and Business Coach | Top Diversity, Inclusion & Culture Expert and Author | Keynote Speaker | Chair Of CIPD Manchester Branch | LinkedIn Creator Accelerator 🌳 FREE DEI Audit Quiz below

### *The About Section: A Story Worth Telling*

Here's where the magic happens. My "About" section doesn't just list achievements; it weaves a narrative.

It's a masterclass in storytelling, where each sentence invites you into my world. I share my journey not just as a career path but as a mission.

I talk about the challenges, the triumphs, and the lessons learned along the way.

It's personal, it's passionate, and it's powerful. It shows that I'm not just working in diversity and inclusion; I'm living it.

### *The Experience Section: The Impact I've Made*

Each position listed is more than a role; it's a chapter in a larger story.

I outline my contributions and achievements, but the focus is always on the impact.

How did I drive change? How did I champion inclusivity? It's all there, detailed in the experience section that paints a picture of a leader who doesn't just do the job but makes a difference.

### *Recommendations: Voices of Validation*

This section is where my influence truly shines.

Colleagues, clients, and peers share their experiences, highlighting my commitment to diversity and inclusivity.

It's one thing to claim these values for myself; it's another to see them reflected in the words of others.

These recommendations serve as a chorus of validation, amplifying my message and my mission.

### *Skills And Endorsements: A Reflection of Expertise*

My skills aren't just a list but a testament to my expertise and focus on inclusivity.

Each endorsement acknowledges my capabilities in my field and my broader mission to drive change.

It shows where my strength lies and what I have achieved in the past. The many endorsements I have been given on each skill further validate my claims and skill.

**Strategic Engagement: Beyond the Surface**

My approach to engagement was strategic, focusing on creating content that served as a magnet for meaningful interactions.

I honed my craft with the help of a LinkedIn coach, focusing on the pillars of hook, story, value, and call to action.

This wasn't just posting for the sake of visibility; I created messages that invited engagement, reflection, and conversation.

**The Impact of Inclusivity**

Overall, my profile is a beacon for potential employers, clients and for anyone looking to make their mark in an inclusive and impactful way.

It demonstrates that success on LinkedIn isn't just about showcasing skills or experiences; it's about showing who you are and what you stand for.

By focusing on diversity and inclusion, I have elevated my presence and set a new standard for what a LinkedIn profile can be.

It's not just a resume; it's a rallying cry, a call to action for us all to be more inclusive, diverse, and impactful in our professional and business journeys.

When crafting a LinkedIn profile, my message is clear: your LinkedIn profile can be more than just a summary of your career.

It can be a declaration of your values, a showcase of your impact, and a testament to the power of inclusivity.

## Key Takeaways for Your LinkedIn Makeover

1. **Authenticity is Magnetic:** Your profile should reflect your professional identity, passions, and values. Authenticity attracts like-minded professionals and opens doors to genuine opportunities. How do you achieve this?

    - **Be True to Your Story:** Start with a personal branding exercise. List down your core values, passions, and the unique perspectives you bring to your industry. Reflect these elements in every section of your profile, from the summary to the experiences, making sure they tell a cohesive story of who you are professionally and personally.

    - **Visual Authenticity:** Use a profile picture and background that reflect your professional background yet show a glimpse of your personality. Consider images that resonate with your professional community or passions, making your first impression memorable.

    - **Share Your Journey:** Regularly post updates, articles, and stories that highlight your successes, challenges, and lessons learned along the way. This could include project milestones, professional insights, or personal development achievements. It's about showing progress, resilience, and the real person behind the profile.

2. **Inclusivity is a Superpower:** Embrace and showcase your commitment to diversity and inclusion. It enriches your profile and positions you as a thought leader in creating equitable professional spaces.

    - **Diversify Your Network:** Actively seek and connect with professionals from various backgrounds, industries, and experiences. This enriches your feed with diverse perspectives and demonstrates your commitment to inclusivity.

    - **Highlight Inclusive Projects and Achievements:** In your experience section and posts, highlight any projects or roles where you've actively contributed to diversity and inclusion. Whether it's leading a diversity initiative, participating in community outreach, or implementing inclusive policies at work, let these efforts shine on your profile.

    - **Engage in Conversations About Inclusivity:** Participate in and initiate discussions on diversity, equity, and inclusion within your industry. Share articles, comment on posts, and engage with content that aligns with these values, positioning yourself as an advocate for inclusivity.

3. **Engagement is Key:** Don't just broadcast; engage. Share insights, ask questions, and participate in discussions. Engagement transforms your profile from a monologue to a dialogue, inviting more connections and opportunities.

    - **Consistent Content Creation:** Develop a content calendar for your LinkedIn activities. Plan regular posts that align with your expertise and interests, and stick to a consistent posting schedule. This could include original articles, curated content relevant to your industry, and personal insights or experiences.
    - **Interactive Posts:** When crafting your posts, include questions or calls to action that encourage your network to engage. Ask for opinions, share polls, or invite comments on a topic. This not only boosts engagement but also fosters a two-way conversation.
    - **Be a Community Participant:** Don't just post; be active in the LinkedIn community. Comment on other people's posts, congratulate connections on their achievements and join industry-relevant groups. Engagement is a two-way street; the more you interact with others, the more visibility and interaction your content will receive.

Remember that the journey doesn't end with a profile update. The platform is always evolving, and so should your LinkedIn presence.

Keep refining, experimenting, and growing as a professional or business owner who stands for authenticity, inclusivity, and engagement.

## Chapter Three

## Content Mastery: M.A.P.P.I.N.G. Your Inclusive Journey to LinkedIn Success

Now you've got your product (knowledge and expertise), but how do you set up your stall to attract the right crowd?

It's not enough just to shout about what you're selling; you need a plan, a strategy that resonates with your audience while championing diversity and inclusivity.

Let's roll up our sleeves and craft a content plan that's as effective as it is inclusive. And what better way to do this than to introduce my unique formula for conversion?

The **LinkedIn M.A.P.P.I.N.G.** Method:

**M - Monitor Trends and Topics:** Keep your finger on the pulse of current discussions and trending topics. Be aware of the evolving conversations in your industry, especially those around diversity and inclusivity.

**A - Authenticity Always:** Your content should reflect your true self. Authenticity fosters trust and credibility, especially when discussing sensitive topics like inclusivity.

**P - Personalise and Participate:** Don't just broadcast; engage. Personalise your interactions and participate in discussions, showing genuine interest in others' perspectives.

**P - Purpose-driven Posting:** Every piece of content should have a purpose, whether it's to inform, inspire, or invite discussion. Ensure that your content contributes positively to the narrative around inclusivity.

**I - Inclusive Insights:** Share insights that embrace and highlight diversity. Your content should reflect a range of voices and perspectives, celebrating differences.

**N - Nurture:** Use your content to build and nurture a diverse network. Connect with people from different backgrounds and foster a community of mutual support.

**G - Goal-oriented Growth:** Tailor your content to support your professional or business goals, but ensure these goals align with promoting diversity and inclusivity within your network.

Now, let's dive into the details.

**Monitoring Trends and Topics** is like having your ear to the ground. What are people talking about? What's missing in the conversation?

For example, if there's a buzz about gender equality in the tech industry, contribute with content that adds value to that discussion, perhaps sharing your own experiences or highlighting success stories of diverse tech leaders. You could add value here by sharing your predictions and unique insights.

To achieve this, you can:

- **Follow Industry Leaders and Influencers:** Keep tabs on thought leaders and influencers in your field, especially those who champion diversity and inclusivity. They often set the tone for industry conversations.
- **Use LinkedIn's 'Trending' Feature:** Regularly check LinkedIn's trending news and hashtags. This helps you stay updated with current discussions and find opportunities to contribute meaningfully.
- **Join Relevant Groups and Forums:** Participate in LinkedIn groups related to your industry and interests. These can be goldmines for fresh ideas, trending topics and paid work.

**Authenticity is your currency on LinkedIn.** People can spot a fake from a mile away. Let it come from your own experiences and beliefs. When you talk about your insights, always have inclusivity in mind. It's like sharing a piece of your heart with your network.

Here's what you can do:

- **Share Personal Stories and Experiences:** People connect with real stories. Share your journey, challenges, and victories related to your career and advocacy for inclusivity.
- **Be Transparent in Your Opinions and Beliefs:** When discussing issues, especially around inclusivity, be clear and honest about where you stand. Authenticity builds trust.
- **Consistently Reflect Your Brand Values:** Ensure your content consistently reflects your personal and professional values, particularly in championing diversity and inclusivity.

**Personalisation and Participation** go hand in hand. It's not just about posting content; it's about engaging with what others post.

Comment on others' posts, offer insights and build genuine connections. It's like mingling at a party instead of just standing in the corner. To make this work:

- **Engage with Comments on Your Posts:** Don't just post and ghost. Actively respond to comments to create a dialogue and show that you value others' opinions. Do so with a 2-hour window for maximum impact and for the algorithm to favour your post.
- **Comment on Others' Posts with Thoughtful Insights:** Make meaningful contributions to others' content. This builds relationships and establishes you as an engaged member of your community.
- **Tailor Your Content to Your Audience's Needs and Interests:** Understand your audience and create content that addresses their specific interests, challenges, and questions.

**Purpose-driven Posting** means every post should serve a goal. The call to action you use at the end of the post should, therefore, tie in with the goal of the post. Whether you're sharing an article on inclusive hiring practices or a personal story about overcoming biases, your content should aim to educate, engage, or empower.

Here's how:

- **Set Clear Objectives for Each Post**: Whether it's to inform, inspire, or engage, define what you want to achieve with each post.
- **Educate Your Audience:** Share insights, tips, and knowledge, especially around inclusivity and diversity, to educate your audience.
- **Create Content that Sparks Discussion:** Pose questions or share viewpoints, encouraging your network to think and engage in conversation.

**Inclusive Insights** are your window to showcase diversity. Share stories and insights that reflect various perspectives. It's like inviting guests from all walks of life to contribute to the rich conversation at your dinner table. You can:

- **Highlight Diverse Perspectives and Voices:** Share content showcasing various viewpoints, especially from underrepresented groups in your industry.
- **Address Inclusivity and Diversity Issues:** Create content that discusses and brings light to inclusivity challenges and solutions in the workplace.
- **Share Success Stories:** Highlight success stories in your business or profession. This gives you the opportunity to show social proof. For example, you can share a written or video

testimonial, (video does better), awards and recognition, highlights of other companies doing great things that align with the work you do.

- **Nurturing** is about growing your LinkedIn family. Connect with people from diverse backgrounds, engage with their content, and support their endeavours. Nurture your audience with content that resonates and reflects inclusive values. Convert not just to leads but to advocates for inclusivity.

- **Regularly Connect with New People:** Continuously expand your network by connecting with people from diverse backgrounds and industries.

- **Offer Help and Support:** Be proactive in offering assistance, advice, or resources to your connections.

- **Create and Participate in Group Discussions:** Engage in or initiate discussions in LinkedIn groups to foster a sense of community and belonging.

**Goal-oriented Growth** is about aligning your content strategy with your career goals, ensuring that your pursuit of professional success goes hand in hand with championing inclusivity. You should therefore:

- **Align Content with Professional or Business Goals:** Make sure your posts contribute to your larger career objectives, such as establishing thought leadership or expanding your professional network.

- **Measure and Adapt:** Regularly review the performance of your posts (engagement, reach, etc.) and adapt your strategy accordingly to achieve your goals.

- **Create a Content Calendar:** Plan your content in advance, ensuring a consistent and strategic approach to your LinkedIn activity.

My LinkedIn **M.A.P.P.I.N.G. The Method** isn't just a formula; it's a commitment to creating a LinkedIn presence that's as inclusive as it is impactful.

By following this framework, you're not just mapping out a content strategy; you're charting a course towards a more inclusive professional and business world, one post at a time.

## Inclusive Content Mapping Case Study: A Journey to Viral Success

Your content plan isn't just a hit-and-miss affair; it needs a calculated, strategic approach to succeed, help you grow and attract a diverse audience.

When it comes to content creation, I leverage various forms of posts, from insightful articles and engaging videos to interactive polls and eye-opening infographics.

Frequency is also crucial. I strike a balance between being present and not overwhelming my audience, opting for quality over quantity.

One of my secret sauces is using LinkedIn's unique features to my advantage. Take LinkedIn polls, for instance. Instead of blatant self-promotion, you can use polls to spark conversations around topics relevant to your niche. These polls not only gauge interest but also open doors to meaningful dialogues.

Another key element is the seamless integration of lead magnets into your content. Whether it's a freebie that solves a common problem or a quiz that offers personalised insights, my content naturally leads the audience to these resources, making the journey from LinkedIn to my email list almost effortless.

The goal of your content plan and strategy is to create a controllable lead flow – a dial you can turn up or down to manage your engagement.

You want to have a consistent presence without overwhelming your audience. Here's how to apply this in practice:

**Quick Wins:** Start with a campaign targeting your existing network. Leverage your connections for quick engagement boosts. It's like rekindling old friendships with a purpose.

**LinkedIn Engagement to Grow, Nurture, Convert:** Grow your network by connecting with new prospects. Nurture them with your content – think of it as gently warming them up to your ideas. Convert by driving them to take action, whether it's joining your email list, signing up for a webinar, or downloading a freebie.

**LinkedIn Lives -** You can use "LinkedIn Lives" as a way to grow your audience too! This also helps to create a deeper connection with your target audience.

**Power Content:** Commit to posting powerful content at least twice a week. These are not just any posts; they are your best, most engaging pieces that spark conversations and build connections.

**Image Posts:** Here, you can also include images to add to your power content arsenal. A picture, they say, speaks volumes. Ensure that 90% of the images in your content are professionally shot. Yes, you can include photos of network events, etc. and can be more relaxed to bring authenticity. Ensure that you add image description/ ALT text this could be done in some schedulers or in LinkedIn when posting directly.

**Conversion Posts:** Use polls, questions, and calls to action to transform engagement into tangible results. It's like having a friendly chat that subtly guides them towards discovering more about you.

**Using Powerful Hooks:** Next, let's take a look at hooks that don't quite hit the mark. The core issue?

It's simple: not enough practice in crafting hooks.

Here's a fresh approach I've been adopting:

Firstly, take a leaf out of the book of viral hooks. Why try to reinvent the wheel when you can learn from the best? When you see a strategy working, model it to see how it works for you.

Secondly, in the initial draft, experiment with three different hooks. It's like a mini-competition where the best one wins.

Lastly, revisit and refine your past hooks. It's a learning curve, and each tweak is a step towards mastery.

As you map out your content plan, remember that each post is a brushstroke in the bigger picture of your professional narrative. Make each one resonate with the spirit of inclusivity.

I'll share some hooks that have really worked for me with amazing results.

Examples include phrases like

- My superpower unleashed ***
- I used this method...
- This changed my life...
- You are gonna want to know this...

For a good hook, you can use storytelling, an unpopular opinion, myth-busting or a surprising stat in your industry. Sharing related tips or tricks also works well.

Hooks to spark conversations:

- What do you think of this?
- What top tip would you add?
- This or that ( comparison)

Hooks within the call to action
- Add your own top tip in comments
- Grab my freebie in comments
- Dm the word " Ready" for a free interview step-by-step guide
- Remember to like, comment and share

Here is a template for your **content pillar**:

- Focus on content that resonates with your target audience. You can opt for topics you can speak about for at least 10 minutes straight
- For example, I focus on:
    - Visibility tips
    - LinkedIn profile tips & hacks
    - Diversity & Inclusion
    - Working Career Mom tips
    - Women accelerating in their careers
    - Representation

Developing your **posting strategy**

- For example:
    - Monday: Thought leadership
    - Tuesday: Invitation
    - Wednesday: Personal Share
    - Thursday: Optional post/off-the-cuff post
    - Friday: Motivation or disruption
    - Saturday: Optional post/off-the-cuff post
    - Sunday: None

- Start by publishing 4-5 posts per week to develop your style, potentially increasing to two posts daily.
- Maintain a consistent posting schedule, ideally early morning (7-9 am Central Time) or late afternoon (4 pm Central Time).
- While you can post any day of the week, aim for consistency on the same days. Optimal days may include Monday, Tuesday, Wednesday, Friday, and Saturday.
- Monitor closely to determine the most effective posting days and times for your audience.
- Ensure a minimum of 90% of your content aligns with your brand, especially if you're monetising on LinkedIn. Always question the relevance of your content to your audience.
- Only use 3 to 5 hashtags max
- Incorporate diversity and inclusion throughout your entire content creation and communication

Now you can have more meaningful conversations with better engagement and keep growing your audience.

## Chapter Four

## Creator Catalyst: Unleashing Profit and Inclusion on LinkedIn

In this chapter, we'll cover how you can unleash your creativity and make some profit while championing inclusivity.

It's like hitting two birds with one stone in the best way possible.

Here are proven strategies that you can use to transform your journey on LinkedIn:

**1. Find Your Unique Voice**

First things first, what makes you, well, you? On LinkedIn, authenticity is your golden ticket, and you must use it to your advantage.

Your experiences, insights, and personal stories? That's gold right there. Share your journey, the ups and the downs. People connect with realness, and that's a big win for inclusivity.

**Actionable Tip:** Start by jotting down what you're passionate about. It could be anything from AI in HR to knitting – whatever floats your boat. Then, think about how these passions have shaped your professional life. Boom – you've got yourself a unique angle.

**2. Embrace Diverse Content Forms**

Don't just stick to text posts. LinkedIn loves variety – think videos, infographics, and even simple illustrations. Each format can reach a different audience segment, promoting inclusivity. Plus, it keeps your content fresh and engaging.

Ensure that inclusion is kept in mind so that you can attract diverse audiences in your niche. Use Closed captions on video - LinkedIn now has auto-captions you can check and approve.

Also, use ALT descriptions in your photo uploads. For example, "A black woman smiling in a multi-colour dress leaning on a window pane."

So when uploading a photo, click on ALT text to add an image description. Then select "Done".

Remember, this allows for inclusivity. It will help those who are blind or partially sighted and use assistive technology to view your content.

ALT Text provides basic or essential information about an image.

Note that ALT text and image descriptions are different - ALT text tells people what is in an image, such as text or basic essential details. If an image fails to load, alt text will display in its place. Search engines also index ALT-text information and consider it a factor when determining search engine ratings.

An image description gives more details than alt text and allows someone to learn more about what is in an image that goes beyond alt text. Alt text gives the user the most important information, while image descriptions provide further detail.

For example, alt text tells someone that there's a puddle on the floor, and image description tells someone that the puddle on the floor is in the middle of the floor and it's orange juice.

**Image Description -** Usually 280 characters or less. More detail than an alt-text

- Include placement, image style, colours, names, animals, clothes (if important detail), emotions, and surroundings.
- Leave out: 'obvious' features e.g. they have a nose and mouth.
- You can add 'null' if your image is purely decorative.

**Use Camel Case -** Camel case is the practice of writing phrases without spaces or punctuation, indicating the separation of words with a single capitalised letter and the first word starting with either case.

Like this
#diversityandinclusion #mentalhealth #disability #workplace #researchandinnovation #freewebinar
or
Like this
#DiversityAndInclusion #MentalHealth #Disability #Workplace #ResearchAndInnovation #FreeWebinar

More examples:

#DiversityAndInclusion

#CareerMum

#EmpowerWomen

**Descriptive Link Text**

Descriptive link text is important for accessibility and usability. Instead of using generic phrases like "click here" or "read more," it's better to use descriptive text that accurately describes where the link leads or what action it performs. This way, users who rely on screen readers or who have difficulty navigating can understand the purpose of the link without needing additional context.

Here, you have a text that describes what a particular link indicates on the page. For example:

- "Click here to read about our company."
- "To learn more about our company, read About Us."

**Actionable Tip:** Experiment with different formats. Try a short video about your latest project, or create an infographic summarising a complex concept you love. Watch what resonates with your audience and refine as you go.

**3. Consistency is Key**

You can't just post once in a blue moon and expect miracles. Set a schedule and stick to it. Consistency builds trust, and trust leads to engagement and, with consistency, profit.

**Actionable Tip:** Pick three days a week to post and stick to them religiously. It doesn't have to be a grand post every time; sometimes, a quick insight or an engaging question works wonders.

I would recommend 6 am - 8 am as high traffic, then the lunch hour 12 pm or the commute times 5 pm or 6 pm. For the weekend, this is optional, as weekdays are known to be more professional.

### 4. Engage Genuinely

Engagement isn't just about getting likes and comments. It's about building a community. Respond to comments, join conversations, and be a part of other users' journeys too.

**Actionable Tip:** Spend 15 minutes a day engaging with other posts. Drop thoughtful comments, not just 'Great post!' Show you've read their content and add your perspective. Be on the platform just before your post is scheduled to go out.

### 5. Leverage LinkedIn Features

LinkedIn constantly rolls out new features, such as LinkedIn Live, Audio, or even good old articles. These can be powerful tools to boost your visibility.

**Actionable Tip:** Host a "LinkedIn Live" session discussing a topic close to your heart. It's a great way to connect in real time and add a personal touch to your digital presence. If you invite guests, remember to bring along diverse perspectives.

### 6. Inclusivity in Action

Remember, inclusivity isn't just a buzzword; it's action. Highlight diverse voices and experiences in your content. Share stories and insights from various industries, cultures, and backgrounds.

**Actionable Tip:** Collaborate with professionals from different fields or backgrounds for a post or a series. It's a great way to broaden your and your audience's perspectives.

### 7. Track and Tweak

What's working? What's not? LinkedIn provides analytics for a reason. Use these insights to understand your audience better and tailor your content accordingly. It is important to check your analytics to help you understand your audience better.

After a post, check to see

- How many likes, comments and shares
- How many impressions
- How many DMs (more important in some niches who may prefer to avoid liking or commenting on your posts this could include professions like counselling, mental health, diversity and inclusion etc.)
- How many followers
- How many profile visits

Define your goals for lead generation. For example, is it to increase sales? To gain brand visibility? etc.

**Actionable Tip:** Once a month, dive into your LinkedIn analytics. Look for patterns – which posts got the most engagement? What time did you post them? Use these insights to inform your future content strategy.

## 8. Stay Updated

LinkedIn, like all social platforms, evolves constantly. Stay on top of trends and updates. This agility will boost your presence and position you as a thought leader.

**Actionable Tip:** Set aside time each week to read up on the latest LinkedIn trends and features. A quick Google search or a scroll through LinkedIn's official blog can do wonders.

## 9. Personalised Outreach

As your network grows, personalised connection requests and messages can make a world of difference. It shows you value the individual, not just the connection count.

**Actionable Tip:** When reaching out to someone, mention something specific from their profile or a post that resonated with you. It shows you're paying attention and not just playing the numbers game.

I recommend you actively go on their profile to see their interests and likes and engage with their post before you connect.

This not only shows interest but also gets you ready to have a value-driven conversation.

There you have it!

Becoming a successful LinkedIn creator isn't just about posting content. You need to build a community, foster inclusivity, and show the world the unique and awesome professional or business owner that you are.

Remember these strategies, and you're well on your way to becoming another LinkedIn success story.

## Creator Spotlight: Realising Profit and Inclusion

LinkedIn creators have used their platforms to achieve remarkable success, blending profitability with a deep commitment to diversity and inclusion. I'll share my journey and the inspiring story of Elaine Hughes, a client whose success story exemplifies the power of targeted and inclusive content strategy.

My journey on LinkedIn started as a simple attempt to connect with other professionals but quickly evolved into a powerful platform for advocacy and business growth. As I began to share more about my experiences and insights into diversity and inclusion, something incredible happened: people listened.

I crafted content that resonated not just with any audience but with those who shared my passion for making the workplace more inclusive. This wasn't about generic posts but about stories that mattered—real, raw, and resonant. The response was overwhelming. Not only did my followers grow, but my posts started to go viral.

But the real success was in the tangible outcomes. More clients began to reach out, drawn by my authentic voice and the results of my inclusive strategies. I gained recognition and won awards. My LinkedIn platform became a lead generator, funnelling interested parties directly to my coaching services and online courses. Each course sold was a testament to the trust and credibility I had built through my content. Every client interaction was an opportunity to practise what I preached: profitability intertwined with inclusivity.

Following the strategies I advocate, my client Elaine Hughes, a Luxury DEI Business Strategist, also transformed her LinkedIn presence into a dynamic tool for change. Working with premium hospitality and event organisers, Elaine focuses on creating inclusive spaces that welcome everyone, especially the often-overlooked Black Disabled Community.

Elaine's success on LinkedIn is not just a matter of posting frequently; it's about posting with purpose. As a Black Disabled Woman, she brings a unique and powerful perspective to the table. Her posts go beyond mere updates; they challenge the status quo and advocate for real, meaningful inclusion in luxury spaces. Her voice amplifies the concerns and aspirations of a community that is frequently marginalised.

The pinnacle of Elaine's LinkedIn achievements came when she received the "Top Voice" recognition within months of consistent posting, which is a prestigious badge given by LinkedIn. This accolade was a direct result of her strategic and passionate use of the platform to speak on issues that matter both to her and to her audience. It's proof that when you speak authentically and from the heart, the impact can be profound.

Elaine offers a range of services aimed at enhancing inclusivity in high-end environments, and her LinkedIn profile serves as a primary channel for client engagement.

For everyone who's been hesitant to share their voice, remember Elaine's and my journeys. We started with a simple desire to make a difference and grew into voices of authority in our fields. LinkedIn is more than a network; it's a platform for change. Use it to shine a spotlight on issues you care about, and you might just find that success on LinkedIn is synonymous with making a real impact.

Scan Here To Follow Elaine Hughes on LinkedIn.

## Chapter Five

# Content Alchemy: Unlocking Profitability and Inclusion on LinkedIn

This chapter will help you transform ordinary updates into captivating, impactful content, unlocking the potential to foster inclusivity and drive profit on your LinkedIn journey.

We'll uncover how to craft captivating content that resonates with a diverse audience and also turns engagement into tangible business success.

## Transforming Content into Profitable Alchemy

Turning your LinkedIn content into a dynamic and profitable tool goes beyond just regular posting. You need to strike the right chord with both inclusivity and revenue generation.

Let's dive into how you can master this alchemy:

**Identify Revenue-Generating Themes**

Understanding what resonates with your audience is key to profitable content. Identify topics closely related to your products or services that interest your audience.

This process involves tuning into the needs and pain points of your network and tailoring your content to address these areas. Focus on topics that align with your products or services.

Next, analyse which posts garner the most client inquiries and push out more related content. Regularly share insights related to your industry's pain points to keep attracting potential clients. Go on to your competitors' profiles; what are they talking about? What comments are coming up? Turn the most popular pain points into a post.

**Create Solution-Oriented Content**

Your content should be a source for the solutions to your audience's challenges. You position yourself as a go-to resource by highlighting how your services or products solve real-world problems.

Share success stories and client testimonials to add credibility and tangible evidence of your expertise.

Frame your content around your solutions and ensure they align naturally and logically. You can use case studies or client testimonials to showcase your success so they can see the possible results or outcomes they'll get when they patronise you.

Craft posts that answer common questions in your field to draw in customers looking for similar solutions.

**Build a Sales Funnel Through Content**

A strategic content plan can gently guide your audience from awareness to purchase. Start with posts that build awareness and gradually introduce your services or products, leading them down a path towards becoming a customer.

Direct followers to lead magnets such as webinars, eBooks, or trials that you provide.

Use calls to action to guide your audience toward purchasing. You need to tell them the exact action to take after consuming your content. For example, *Sign up now*, *Download here*, and so on.

This prompts them to move in the direction you want to go for the next steps in your funnel. If you leave this out, you might lose some clients as they would leave after consuming your content.

The overall picture here is to create content that starts with a hook, leads into a valuable story, and ends with a call to action.

**Leverage LinkedIn's Features for Maximum Reach**

Making the most of LinkedIn's unique features can amplify your content's impact. From stories to live sessions, each tool offers a different way to engage with your audience and expand your reach. Tailor your content to these formats for maximum effectiveness.

Use LinkedIn Stories and Live sessions to promote real-time interactions and to reach new audiences.

Ensure that you optimise your posts for SEO by using relevant keywords so that your posts will show up when people search for keywords relating to you on LinkedIn. This gives you the opportunity to reach people who are actively seeking what you offer. A term known as "hot leads". If done right, these sets of clients are easier to convert into paying customers.

Experiment with different content formats to see what drives the most engagement.

**Engage and Convert Your Network**

Engagement is the cornerstone of conversion on LinkedIn. Building relationships with your connections can turn them from passive followers into active customers. Personalised follow-ups and responses to their needs are crucial in this process.

Actively engage with your connections and respond to their needs or questions they have asked.

Use personalised messages to follow up on engagement and build meaningful relationships.

You can also reach out directly to potential clients via direct messaging on LinkedIn. When reaching out, ensure that you do your research. Avoid sending generic messages.

One last tip for this section is to offer exclusive discounts or services to your LinkedIn network. That way, your profile will attract new audiences and keep growing your reach.

**Host Value-Driven Events**

Events are a powerful way to provide concentrated value to your network._ Hosting webinars, live Q&A sessions, or partnering with other influencers at events can showcase your expertise and attract potential clients.

Organise webinars or live Q&A sessions focusing on solving specific problems for your target audience. You can also partner with other LinkedIn influencers to expand your reach.

Remember to use these events as an opportunity to subtly pitch your product or services.

**Track, Analyse, and Optimise for Profit**

Data-driven adjustments are key to content success. By understanding what types of content yield the best results, you can fine-tune your strategy to focus on the most profitable avenues, ensuring a higher return on your investment.

You need to check your post analytics regularly to understand what's working to achieve this. Next, adjust your strategy based on engagement and conversion data and invest more in content types and topics that generate the highest ROI.

**Incorporate Inclusive and Diverse Perspectives**

Inclusivity in content broadens your reach and strengthens your brand. Ensuring your content speaks to a wide range of experiences and perspectives can deepen your connection with a diverse audience.

You can highlight diverse case studies or stories that resonate with various groups and tie the story or case study to your product or service.

Don't forget to use inclusive language and visuals that reflect a range of experiences.

**Monetise Your Expertise**

Your knowledge and experience are valuable commodities on LinkedIn. Positioning yourself as a thought leader and offering your expertise through consultations or exclusive content can open new revenue streams for you.

You can offer paid consultations or exclusive content for a fee. This can be set up using simple tools like Calendly for bookings.

Your knowledge and expertise can also be shared through courses or workshops, which you can promote within your profile to generate additional income.

**Nurture Long-Term Client Relationships**

Fostering ongoing client relationships is crucial to sustainable success. Use your content to keep them informed, engaged, and connected to your brand, thus ensuring they remain loyal and possibly even advocate for your services.

Share regular updates about your business and industry to maintain relevance and be top of their minds.

Offer special deals or content exclusively for long-term clients to make them feel special.

## Planning Your Content

There are different categories that you can use to plan your content. Here is a quick idea for your content category that you can use:

- **Thought leadership** - This involves offering worthwhile advice, resources, and ideologies that are specific to your area of expertise.
- **Motivation and disruption** - This encompasses empowering affirmations, meaningful quotations, and proactive calls to action that resonate with the aspirations of your perfect audience while challenging unproductive thoughts related to your sector.
- **Promotional posts** - This is aimed at highlighting your services or products with the goal of cultivating leads and boosting sales.
- **Personal branding posts -** This involves revealing brand narratives and lifestyle-related content to foster a stronger bond with your audience.

Balancing valuable, inclusive content with strategies that directly contribute to your bottom line is essential in mastering the art of turning LinkedIn content into a profitable tool. Following these steps can transform your content from mere posts into a powerful, revenue-generating asset.

## Alchemy Success Stories: A Blend of Profit and Inclusion

Gaining traction on LinkedIn takes a lot of effort. But if you do the work, then you are bound to reap the rewards.

Many professional and business owners have successfully used the platform to grow and you can do the same.

To grow and be profitable on LinkedIn, you need to be intentional when connecting and engaging.

Reaching out to new connections is good, but you have to be strategic about it.

Here is an example of a direct message I received in my inbox:

> Hey Samantha, glad to be connected here. Happy New Year!
>
> I checked on your profile, and you're up to awesome things.
>
> For how long have you been coaching?

This is a style I would not encourage because people will not respond to this. They know that it's just disingenuous.

The message comes across as generic, but it has one good point: "I checked your profile," which is nice.

I recommend that you point out something that I've said that you admire or like and don't ask, "How long have you been coaching?"

If proper research were done, it would be obvious that I don't talk much about my coaching on my profile, and that is also not the major thing I do.

On my page, I talked mostly about women and inequality. The fact that it was not mentioned shows that no research was done and that my profile was not even checked.

This kind of message is often sent to multiple people while hoping for a bite. Now, it may work for some people, and it seems like an easy thing to do, but only if you want short-term results.

However, if you want long-term, long-standing relationships with people, real connections, genuine connections to build trust, and authentic relationships, then you need to do the legwork.

Here is another example of what not to do!

> Hassnain unsent a message
>
> Hi client name! 😊
> I resonate with your presence on your Facebook/LinkedIn profile immensely! I wish you all the success for the new year.
> Just a quick question as I know you must be working on a busy schedule and getting a lot of offers from start-ups these days which has been quite annoying in our industry over the past few months, if you can relate?

Clearly, this is an indication that a template was used, and the "CLIENT name" left in there shows that he forgot to update his template, which was designed for two different platforms (Facebook/LinkedIn)

Now compare these with the example below:

 ~~Saurin Asady~~ (The LinkedIn Coach) • 10:57 PM
Hey Samantha, I eat, sleep, and breathe LinkedIn!

I always share content and strategies to get more clients using LinkedIn effectively.

If you like that kind of content, let's connect!

This comes across as friendly and may convert better as it highlights a possible pain point however it fails to show interest in the individual you are connecting with as a person and it is not personalised.

When utilising LinkedIn for networking, it's essential to approach each connection with a genuine interest in developing meaningful relationships. Instead of simply promoting your own agenda, focus on building rapport by expressing curiosity about the other person's background, experiences, and goals.

For instance, if you come across someone who works in a complementary industry, rather than immediately pitching your services or products, take the time to learn about their work and how it aligns with yours. You might discover potential collaboration opportunities, such as joint projects or events that could benefit both parties.

Similarly, when connecting with individuals in your local area, explore ways to support each other's endeavours. This could involve attending local networking events together, sharing resources or contacts, or even collaborating on community initiatives.

Furthermore, consider reaching out to individuals who have connections in your target market or industry. Instead of solely focusing on what they can do for you, strive to establish mutually beneficial relationships by offering assistance, insights, or introductions that could be valuable to them as well.

By approaching LinkedIn connections with a genuine interest in building meaningful partnerships and offering mutual support, you'll not only expand your network but also lay the foundation for long-term professional and long term financial success.

**Now, below I share my Connect to Covert 5 STEP method:**

**Step 1: Engage with Their Profile**

Start by visiting their LinkedIn profile. Show genuine interest by liking and commenting on posts that resonate with you. This initial engagement is crucial as it sets the stage for a personal connection and shows that you are genuinely interested in what they have to say or offer.

**Step 2: Connect with a Personalised Message**

After engaging with their content, send a connection request. Include a personalised message in your request, mentioning something specific you liked or commented on their profile. For example, "I really appreciate your insights on the Equal Pay Act and agree that more action is needed in this area. Thanks for sharing!"

**Step 3: Initiate a Conversation**

Once they accept your connection request, start a conversation by referencing something specific from their profile or your previous interactions.

Keep this interaction light and focused on building rapport. The goal here is to establish a genuine connection, not to sell.

**Step 4: Offer Value**

After a couple of days of conversation and once a level of comfort is established, introduce a resource that might be of value to them, such as a webinar or a lead magnet.

Ask if they'd like the link before sending it to respect their space and avoid appearing pushy. For example, "I have a resource that I believe could really help with some of the challenges you mentioned. Would you like me to send you the link?"

**Step 5: Follow Up and Propose a Next Step**

Follow up a few days later to check if they've accessed the resource. If it's a downloadable item, give them about a week to go through it.

Based on their feedback, you can suggest a discovery call or another form of deeper engagement. For instance, "I saw you signed up for the webinar, and I hope you found it useful. Would you be open to a call to discuss how we can apply some of these strategies directly to your business?"

This process ensures that you're not just reaching out cold but are building a relationship based on mutual interests and respect, gradually leading them from a simple LinkedIn connection to a potential client or collaborator.

I would not recommend using a template however, here's a guide on what you can say in direct messages (DMs) on LinkedIn for better results:

1. **Personalised Introduction**: Start by addressing the person by their name and mentioning something specific from their profile that caught your attention or sparked your interest.

2. **Express Interest**: Express genuine interest in the person's background, experiences, or achievements. Compliment them on a recent accomplishment or project they've worked on.

3. **Common Ground:** Find common ground or shared interests that you can reference in your message. This could be mutual connections, shared experiences, or similar career paths.

4. **Value Proposition:** Briefly explain how connecting with them could be mutually beneficial. Highlight what you bring to the table and how you could potentially collaborate or support each other (This is not sells pitch in the first interactions)

5. **Call to Action**: End your message with a clear call to action, such as inviting them to connect, suggesting a meeting or call to discuss potential opportunities, or asking for their thoughts on a relevant topic.

6. **Polite Closure**: Close your message with a polite closing statement, such as thanking them for their time or expressing your excitement about the possibility of connecting further.

Remember to keep your message concise, professional, and respectful of the recipient's time. Personalising your message and focusing on building a genuine connection will increase the likelihood of a positive response.

## Chapter Six

## Engagement Elevator: Maximising Your LinkedIn Post Impact

This chapter is about creating deep connections and engaging with your audience. So, are you ready to take your LinkedIn engagement to the next level?

It's time to step onto the Engagement Elevator, where we're not just aiming for likes; we're aiming for connections, conversations, and conversions.

There are several effective strategies that you can use, but you need to start with a couple to avoid being overwhelmed. Picking the strategies one after the other will also help you monitor the one giving you the best result.

To truly make an impact with your posts, you need more than just content; you need a strategy that resonates, engages, and converts. Each of these ten steps is a floor on our journey upward, offering unique vantage points to maximise your LinkedIn post impact.

Let's delve into these strategies that can help your LinkedIn posts achieve maximum impact.

### Crafting Irresistible Hooks

Your opening lines are like the welcoming mat of your post. To grab attention, start with something that makes your audience pause and think, "I need to read more."

Ask a thought-provoking question, share a startling fact, stat, myth, or begin with a snippet of a compelling story. You can also use something with value or a tip as your hook - Always think "what's in it for them?".

Imagine starting a post with, "Last year, I turned a major failure into my biggest success. Here's how..."

This kind of opening immediately piques interest and sets the stage for an engaging story. Hooks that start with a personal revelation or a surprising fact can make your audience eager to read on.

Remember, your hook should resonate with your audience's interests and challenges, pulling them in with the promise of valuable insights or solutions.

### Telling Engaging Stories

Stories aren't just for bedtime; they're powerful tools in the professional world, too. A good story on LinkedIn can illustrate your expertise, share your journey, or convey complex ideas in an accessible way.

When crafting your narrative, focus on relatability and emotion.

For instance, "The first time I pitched a major client, I was met with a hard no. Here's how I turned that rejection into a contract..." This approach humanises you and provides valuable lessons to your readers.

You can share personal experiences, professional challenges, or successes in a way that your audience can connect with, learn from, and remember.

**Using Impactful Visuals**

Our brains are wired to respond better to visuals, especially in this digital age. Incorporating eye-catching images or graphics in your posts can significantly increase engagement. Go beyond stock photos; use visuals that add real value to your content.

Let's say you specialise in sustainable business practices. Share a before-and-after image of a workspace you helped transform into an eco-friendly environment.

Accompany it with a caption explaining the changes made and their impact.

This visual representation demonstrates your expertise and communicates the tangible benefits of sustainable practices, making your post more engaging and memorable.

Whether it's a chart that breaks down data, an infographic summarising key points, or a personal photo that illustrates your story, make sure it's relevant and adds to the narrative.

**Encouraging Interaction**

Engagement is a two-way street. To turn your posts into conversations, invite your audience to participate. End with a question, a call-to-action, or a thought-provoking statement that encourages responses.

Encourage and spark conversations with simple phrases like "what additional tip would you add?"

For example, let's say your post is about leadership; you can end the post with, "What's the one leadership lesson you swear by? Drop it in the comments!"

This invites your audience to share their experiences, turning your post into a lively discussion forum. Become part of the crowd:

- Be someone they can reach out to.
- Hear what's bugging them.
- Tailor your services or products as solutions to their problems.

Solve their issues, and they'll help solve your financial ones.

Remember, it takes a human touch to truly connect with humans.

When people comment, engage with them, respond to their comments, ask follow-up questions, and appreciate their input. This will not only boost engagement for your posts but also build relationships.

**Timing Your Posts Strategically**

Posting when your audience is most active is crucial. You can use LinkedIn's analytics to understand when your connections are online and target that time frame for your posts.

For instance, if you notice more activity on your profile on Tuesdays around 10 a.m., schedule your most important content for that time. Monitoring engagement patterns and adapting your posting schedule accordingly can significantly boost interaction.

Experiment by posting at different times and days to determine the sweet spot for your content. Remember, consistency is key – if your audience knows when to expect your posts, they're more likely to engage.

**Maximising LinkedIn's Unique Features**

LinkedIn offers various features like polls, stories, and articles that can enhance your content strategy.

Polls are great for quick engagement and gathering audience insights. Stories can add a personal touch, showcasing the human side of your professional brand.

Imagine you're a career coach. You could host a LinkedIn Live session sharing tips for acing job interviews, then follow up with a poll asking your audience about their biggest interview challenges.

You can use the 'Featured' section to showcase testimonials from successful clients.

Post an article about career development trends directly on LinkedIn, enhancing your position as a thought leader.

Finally, engage in relevant LinkedIn Groups by contributing valuable insights, thereby expanding your reach.

Regularly explore and use these features to keep your content dynamic and engaging.

**Collaborating with Others**

Collaboration can exponentially increase your content's reach. By tagging relevant connections or influencers (with their consent of course), you get to tap into their networks as well.

Consider collaborative posts, interviews, or content series.

Collaboration multiplies your impact.

You can co-author a post with a colleague in a complementary field, tag a mentor in a post thanking them for their guidance, or interview an industry leader and share the insights.

Ensure that these collaborations provide mutual value to get people to participate.

Remember, the key to successful collaboration is relevance and mutual benefit – make sure your combined efforts provide value to both your audiences and includes diverse perspectives.

**Prioritising Quality Over Quantity**

When creating content, it is better to post less frequently with high-quality valuable content than to bombard your audience with mediocre posts.

Invest time crafting posts that offer insights, solutions, or perspectives unique to your expertise. Quality content establishes your credibility and keeps your audience coming back for more.

**Staying Authentic**

Lastly, authenticity is your golden ticket. Be true to who you are and what you stand for. Authentic content creates genuine connections.

Share your successes and your struggles. People resonate with honesty and vulnerability. Authenticity makes it possible to share relatable content, which leads to building trust and credibility in your professional network. Here are some quick tips for staying authentic:

- Think it, then ink it. Write as the thoughts come to you.
- Skip the lengthy explanations. Get straight to the point.
- Chat, don't lecture. Use a tone like you're talking to a friend.
- Picture one person you're speaking to. It makes your message more personal.
- Show a bit of your true self. We're all a little imperfect, and that's okay.

Each strategy is a step closer to boosting likes, comments and cultivating a community around your brand. The goal is to create meaningful connections and position yourself as a leader in your field.

Remember, LinkedIn isn't just about throwing your content into the void and hoping for the best. You must engage with your network, interact, and keep the conversations going.

Here's the thing—authenticity wins every time. So, ditch that salesy vibe and keep it real. And hey, I know hashtags are tempting, but let's not turn our posts into a hashtag soup, okay? Also, a little secret? Trying to outsmart LinkedIn's algorithm doesn't really pay off. Keep your content genuine instead of relying on AI to do the job.

Comparing your LinkedIn growth to others is like comparing apples and oranges—your journey is yours alone, unique and invaluable.

Love and enjoy the platform. LinkedIn isn't just a tool; it's a rhythm, a part of your daily routine. Embrace it, have fun with it, and let your passion shine through. Trust me, when you genuinely enjoy the process, it shows—and your network will feel it, too.

Be consistent with your strategy for at least three months. You will see a significant transformation in your LinkedIn presence. and you're bound to see a significant transformation in your LinkedIn presence.

For those of you waiting for the 'perfect moment' to dive in, guess what? The perfect time is right now. Let's make the most of it together!

## Elevated Engagement Case Study: From Likes to Leads

LinkedIn, when used correctly, can create endless opportunities to potentially pivot a career or catalyse a business opportunity.

This section uncovers the stories of individuals who have transformed simple engagements into substantial business leads,

Let me start with a standout case study of Veronica Owusu, a student who danced her way to LinkedIn success.

Veronica, known on LinkedIn as the "V-Power Coach," embodies a success story that many dream about but few manage to realise. A supernova catalyst, bestselling author, and a vivacious free spirit, Veronica has skillfully merged her personal passions with her professional expertise to create a magnetic LinkedIn presence.

**What's her strategy?**

Veronica's journey on LinkedIn is nearly a decade long, marked by a strategic approach to building and nurturing her network. She has used the platform to showcase her skills and genuinely connect and create value for her audience—coaches and consultants looking to become specialists in their fields through unique online programmes and courses.

**Achievements Unlocked:**

Her engagement strategy and optimised profile have opened numerous doors:

- **Recognition:** Veronica was voted as one of LinkedIn's Top 50 Most Impactful Leaders in 2021.
- **Impactful Partnerships:** Her work includes partnerships with prestigious organisations like the United Nations Industrial Development Organisation (UNIDO) to develop Gender Lens Investing programmes.
- **Leadership Roles:** She has taken on roles such as the President at Educational Communities Worldwide, aiding under-resourced students in Ghana.
- **Speaking Engagements**: Her dynamic presence has made her a sought-after keynote speaker at various events.

Holistic Success through Clarity:

What Veronica credits for her multifaceted success on LinkedIn is clarity:

- **Self-Understanding:** She has a profound clarity on who she is beyond professional labels, integrating her love for dance and personal stories into her brand.
- **Client Focus:** Her deep understanding of her dream clients helps her remain focused on solving specific problems and enriching their transformational journeys.
- **Confident Methodology:** Veronica's clear and confident approach in her methodology ensures that she delivers results for her clients, which in turn perpetuates further success.
- **Purpose-Driven:** At the core of her strategy is a clear understanding of her purpose, which guides all her actions and communications on LinkedIn.

**Engagement and Authenticity:**

By embracing her authentic self and consistently showing up with transparency and empathy, Veronica has built a robust community of over 34,000 followers. Her ability to connect on a personal level through "EDUtainment"—educating through entertainment—has not only fostered meaningful relationships but also attracted numerous paid opportunities for collaboration and growth.

**The Golden Nugget:**

Veronica's story culminates in a powerful message: "Dare to be YOU and shimmer your gold dust to brighten up the world." This encapsulates her philosophy of personal authenticity as a cornerstone of professional success on LinkedIn.

**Insights for LinkedIn Success**

Veronica's story is more than just inspiring—it's instructive. For LinkedIn users, both professional and business owners, wondering how to convert likes and comments into leads and lucrative connections, the answer lies in a blend of authenticity, strategic clarity, and consistent engagement.

Her approach demonstrates that when you know yourself and your audience and you communicate with passion and clarity, LinkedIn is not just a network—it's a stage for success.

Scan Here to Follow Veronica on LinkedIn.

Another standout story comes from a client who experienced a dramatic turnaround in her career prospects simply through strategic profile optimisation.

After a detailed consultation and revamping her LinkedIn profile to highlight her skills, experience, and professional aspirations more clearly, the results were nothing short of spectacular.

Within just a few weeks, she reported receiving more than six job inquiries each day from recruiters who had begun to reach out proactively.

The precision in her profile's language and the strategic use of keywords tailored to her industry not only increased her visibility but also aligned her with her dream job, which she secured shortly thereafter.

The narrative continues with professionals in the business and HR consulting sectors. One such HR consultant experienced immediate benefits from optimising their LinkedIn profile.

The day after implementing the changes suggested during our consultation, they started receiving inquiries about their services. This quick influx of interest led to secured contracts and expanded business opportunities.

This example highlights the direct correlation between a well-crafted LinkedIn presence and professional opportunities. It demonstrates that an effective profile does more than present your qualifications—it actively works for you, attracting the right kind of attention and opening doors to new possibilities.

## The Impact of Strategic Profile Optimisation

These stories collectively illustrate a critical point: optimising your LinkedIn profile is not merely a cosmetic update; it's a strategic move that can lead to substantial career and business advancements.

When you fine-tune various elements within your profile—from the headline and summary to the detailed descriptions of your experiences—you transform your LinkedIn into a dynamic asset that actively contributes to your professional growth.

You can take advantage of the one month free trial LinkedIn offers, but ensure that you have a strategy in place ready to execute.

**Key Takeaways**

- **Visibility Leads to Opportunity:** A well-optimised profile increases your visibility to key decision-makers, recruiters, and potential clients who are actively searching for talents and services that align with what you offer.
- **Less Effort, More Results**: Once your profile is optimised, it does much of the heavy lifting for you, drawing in opportunities naturally and frequently without the constant need for active outreach or promotion.
- **Immediate and Long-Term Benefits:** The effects of profile optimisation can be immediate, as seen in the HR consultant's experience, but also have a lasting impact, as demonstrated by the sustained increase in job inquiries and secured opportunities.
- **A Showcase of Your Professional Narrative:** An optimised LinkedIn profile effectively narrates your professional story, highlighting your strengths, achievements, and the unique qualities that make you an ideal candidate or partner.

You should note that LinkedIn favours posts from its Premium members, and you will notice the difference in your progress when you sign up for Premium.

Based on my experience, I've found that investing in premium memberships significantly enhances performance on LinkedIn. If you're a professional aiming to maximise your impact on the platform, I strongly recommend starting with a LinkedIn Premium account. This level of subscription can greatly increase your opportunities, especially as you're establishing yourself.

However, as your business begins to grow and gain traction—once you have validated your programme or services—it might be beneficial to consider upgrading to Sales Navigator. This advanced option allows you to cast a wider net and target your ideal audience more precisely, potentially leading to more paid opportunities.

There's no need to rush into advanced options if you're new to LinkedIn. Initially, it's important to familiarise yourself with the platform. Start with the Premium account, and as you become more comfortable and see your efforts paying off, you can think about moving to Sales Navigator to further enhance your reach and effectiveness.

LinkedIn offers various Premium account packages designed to cater to diverse professional needs, ranging from individual career advancement to comprehensive business and recruitment operations.

The **LinkedIn Premium Career package** is ideal for job seekers and professionals eager to increase their visibility to recruiters. It includes access to profile viewer insights over the last 365 days, 5 InMail credits per month, unlimited access to LinkedIn Learning, and applicant insights, enhancing the chances of getting hired quickly.

For sales professionals and business owners focused on lead generation, the **LinkedIn Premium Business Package**, offers 15 InMail credits, unlimited people browsing, and vital business insights, making it suitable for those needing advanced browsing capabilities and analytical insights.

The **Sales Navigator Core**, targets sales teams and small business owners. It provides 50 InMail credits, advanced search filters, a sales spotlight, and regular lead recommendations, supporting extensive outreach and lead generation activities.

Geared towards larger sales teams that require more sophisticated sales tools, the **Sales Navigator Advanced package**. It builds on the Core features by adding LinkedIn Teamlink, Smartlinks for enhanced outreach tracking, and advanced reporting to improve collaboration and outreach efforts.

**Sales Navigator Advanced Plus** offers custom pricing for enterprise sales teams with advanced CRM integration needs. This package includes all the benefits of the Advanced package along with deeper CRM integrations, making it ideal for large enterprises needing extensive data syncing and collaboration tools.

**LinkedIn Recruiter Lite**, suits HR professionals and business owners with small to mid-scale hiring needs. It provides 30 InMails per user each month, advanced search filters, unlimited browsing up to third-degree connections, and is geared towards teams needing basic recruiting features without ATS integration.

Finally, the **LinkedIn Recruiter Package**, is tailored for large staffing firms and corporate companies with extensive hiring requirements. It includes up to 150 InMails per month, bulk messaging capabilities, exclusive data ownership, and ATS integration with over 28 tools, streamlining large-scale recruitment processes and enhancing collaborative efforts.

Through these narratives, the chapter not only aims to inspire but also to instruct. It encourages readers to view their LinkedIn profiles as pivotal tools in their professional arsenals.

By applying the lessons from these stories, readers can learn to harness the full potential of their LinkedIn presence, turning simple profile views into career-defining or business opportunities.

# Chapter Seven

# Algorithm Decoded: Demystifying LinkedIn for Optimal Reach

Imagine this: You have just created and posted a brilliant LinkedIn post, but it feels like it vanished into thin air, unseen by even your most loyal followers within their feed. This is not unusual. It is just the algorithm at work.

Many struggle to crack the code of the LinkedIn algorithm, leaving them feeling like they're shouting into the void. But what if you could understand and decode the algorithm and get your posts out to its full potential? How do some posts become the talk of the town while others fade into the background unnoticed? It all comes down to understanding the mysterious ways of the LinkedIn algorithm. Let's demystify this digital mystery together.

## Deciphering the LinkedIn Algorithm

Think of the LinkedIn algorithm as a busy matchmaker, constantly trying to introduce users to content they'll likely fall in love with. It's not just throwing things at the wall to see what sticks. Instead, it's meticulously sorting through posts, looking for that special spark to ignite engagement.

The algorithm favours interactions over the content itself. It's all about how people react to what you post. Do they like it, comment on it, share it? LinkedIn's algorithm also loves posts that spark conversations. So, if your content gets people talking, it's a surefire way to be a favourite on the platform.

So, here's the scoop: LinkedIn's algorithm not only values engagement on your posts but also the time people spend viewing them known as "Linger" time. Plus, it takes into account if they wander over to your profile and stick around there as well.

The more they interact, then the more they linger - (another code for staying on the platform as long as possible), the more your content gets seen.

Beyond just engagement and profile views, It's like your content is auditioning for more screen time, and every interaction is a thumbs-up from the audience.

When you post is just as important as what you post. Hit the stage when your audience is most attentive. For most professionals and business owners, that's during the work week, early mornings or lunch hours. Posting on a lazy Sunday? It might just slip through the cracks.

Ever notice how some faces seem more familiar than others? That's the algorithm at work, too, boosting content from those who show up regularly. By posting consistently, you're not just a passing acquaintance; you become a part of the community's daily routine.

Here's a twist - while posting regularly is important, quality trumps all. The algorithm is smarter than it looks, picking up on cues that indicate whether your content genuinely resonates with people.

Are your posts thoughtful? Do they spark meaningful conversations? If yes, you're on the right track because these are the indicators triggered by the algorithm to keep increasing the visibility of your post.

The algorithm also looks at past interactions. If your network frequently engages with your content, your new posts are more likely to appear in their feeds. It's like having a fan club where members are more likely to see and cheer for your performances.

**Embracing the Algorithm**

Now that we've pulled back the curtain, how can you use this knowledge to your advantage? It's simpler than you might think. Here's how:

- **Diversify Your Content:** Use a mix of videos, images, and text. Each type has its charm and reach, so play to a diverse gallery.
- **Encourage Conversations:** Craft your posts to invite comments. Ask questions, seek opinions, and stir discussions. It's not just about broadcasting but building a dialogue.
- **Post with Purpose and Timing:** Align your posting times with when your audience is most active. Experiment with different times and days to find your sweet spot.
- **Nurture Your Network:** Regularly engage with your connections' content. comment, share, and interact authentically. It's about promoting your content and being a vibrant community member.

Now, let's put this into a practical context.

Imagine you're a career coach who wants to maximise the visibility and engagement of a LinkedIn post. Here's how you might apply the insights from the LinkedIn algorithm to your advantage:

**Example Of A LinkedIn Post Strategy**

**Post Type and Content**

You decide to create a short, engaging video where you discuss the top five mistakes people make on their CV. The informative video ends with a question: "What's the one thing you wish you knew about CV writing before you started your job search?"

**Why This Works:**

- **Engagement-Driven Content:** The video format is more likely to catch the eye and keep users on the platform longer than a simple text post. Plus, it allows for personal expression and connection.
- **Interactive Element:** Ending with a question encourages viewers to comment, boosting the post's visibility due to increased engagement.

**Timing and Frequency**

You post the video on a Tuesday morning around 8 am when you've noticed many of your connections are active online based on previous engagement metrics.

**Why This Works:**

- **Optimal Timing:** Posting during a high-activity window increases the chances of your video being seen and interacted with shortly after posting, which is crucial for gaining initial traction.

**Engagement Practices**

After posting, you stay active on LinkedIn for 20 to 30 minutes, responding to comments and engaging with other posts. This not only boosts your post's activity but also keeps you visible in your connections' feeds.

**Why This Works:**

- **Immediate Interaction:** Quick responses to comments can spark further conversation, keeping your posts active. This ongoing activity signals to LinkedIn that your content is engaging, which may help extend its reach.

**Network Interaction**

Leading up to your video post, you spend several minutes actively commenting on and sharing content from a select group of LinkedIn users who are also in the career development field and are embracing diversity and inclusion.

**Why This Works:**

**Strengthened Network Ties:** You foster reciprocal engagement by supporting your peers' content. Your active participation in their content increases the likelihood they'll check out and engage with your posts, further boosting your content's visibility through their networks.

When you understand and leverage the elements of the LinkedIn algorithm, you can strategically enhance the reach and impact of your posts, making your LinkedIn activity more effective and aligned with your professional or business goals.

# Chapter Eight

# Link Power: Effectively Promoting External Links on LinkedIn

Now you've got valuable resources on your website/blog or want to promote a course, product or webinar. How do you drive your LinkedIn audience there without getting lost in the noise?

This chapter delves into the art of promoting external links on LinkedIn, ensuring they reach as many eyes as possible for maximum impact.

## Strategic Link Promotion: Unlocking External Link Power

Think about the last time you clicked a link in someone's post. What compelled you to take that action? Was it curiosity, the promise of value, or perhaps a blend of both? Understanding the psychology behind why people click can transform your approach to sharing external links.

Let's take a closer look at how the LinkedIn algorithm works.

### Understanding LinkedIn's Attitude Towards External Links

First up, it's crucial to know that LinkedIn, like many social platforms, prefers to keep users on the LinkedIn platform. It's kind of like a party host who wants you to stay and mingle rather than head to another party.

Posts with external links tend to have reduced visibility compared to content kept within LinkedIn. But that doesn't mean you can't use links; you just have to be smarter about how you share them.

So, what should you do?

You need to provide value before sharing the Link.

The straightforward approach of dropping a link right in your post might not be your best move.

Instead, think about weaving your links into your content more subtly.

Start by adding value upfront with a compelling post and teasing the link in the comments. Or better yet, start a discussion and offer the link as a resource in response to inquiries or engagement.

This strategy turns your post into a bustling forum, not just a one-way street.

**Enhance Link Visibility Through Engaging Content**

Imagine you're sharing a pivotal article or your latest blog post. Don't just post the link. Introduce it with a hook that captures the essence of why your network needs to see this.

Maybe it's a groundbreaking idea or a solution to a common problem. Ask your audience a thought-provoking question related to the article or share a powerful quote from it.

You're not just sharing a link; you're starting a conversation.

**Use Rich Media to Highlight the Link**

A picture speaks a thousand words, right? When you want to draw attention to an external article or webpage, consider sharing an image or graphic from the content, or create your own that highlights the key message or data point.

Then, guide your audience to the link in the comments or even better, encourage them to connect with you via direct message to get the link.

Example

DM "Insight" and I will share straight to your inbox.

This approach adds an extra layer of interaction, turning passive viewers into active participants.

**Leverage Articles and LinkedIn Features**

LinkedIn's own features can be powerful allies. Publishing an article directly on LinkedIn that summarises or complements your external content can keep your audience engaged within the platform while still driving them to your external site.

It's like giving them a taste of the cake before directing them to the bakery.

Plus, articles published on LinkedIn often receive wider visibility, boosting your profile and credibility.

**Take Advantage of Newsletters**

LinkedIn allows you to send out newsletters to your audience and this can help you boost engagement for your resources.

Newsletters - go straight into the inboxes of those that subscribe making this is a powerful way to connect and share your external resources.

**Build Relationships Through Strategic Networking**

Ever considered the power of indirect link promotion? To achieve this, you need to engage with other users who share or comment on related topics and when the moment is right, introduce your link as a resource. It's about building relationships, not just broadcasting links.

This kind of genuine interaction can lead to more meaningful exchanges and higher engagement, paving the way for your links to be welcomed, not overlooked.

**Follow-Up Post**

Consider a follow-up post closer to the event date. This time, use a video where you briefly discuss what attendees can expect to learn from the webinar and how it will address their challenges. This adds a personal touch and can significantly boost engagement and interest.

**Strategic Placement of Links**

Ensure that you place your webinar registration link in the comments rather than in the main post. This can help your post reach more of your network, as LinkedIn tends to favour posts without direct external links in the feed.

**Example of Effective Link Promotion**

Let's say you've just written a groundbreaking article on the future of diversity in tech. Instead of just posting the link, you could start with a post like:

"Diversity in tech is more than just a slogan - it's the key to innovation. What's one barrier we need to break to truly open the doors of opportunity? Let's discuss!"

Engage with the comments, and then drop the link saying:

"These insights are fantastic! I've explored these barriers and potential solutions in depth in my latest article. If you're looking for more detailed strategies and real-world examples, check out the link in the first comment below."

Let's explore another practical scenario for promoting an external link effectively on LinkedIn, focusing on a common challenge many professionals face: promoting a webinar.

Here's another example for sharing a link to your webinar:

Suppose your webinar is about innovative strategies for remote team management. Your post could look something like this:

"Managing remote teams has its own set of challenges and rewards. What's the biggest hurdle you've faced with remote management, and how did you overcome it?"

Before dropping the link, engage with your audience. Respond to comments with insights and further questions to deepen the discussion. This builds interest and anticipation for your webinar.

After a lively discussion, introduce your webinar as a valuable resource. For example:

"Thank you for sharing your experiences and challenges managing remote teams! To dive deeper into effective strategies and real-life case studies, I'm hosting a webinar this Friday. I believe it will provide some actionable solutions to many of the issues we've discussed. Check out the link in the first comment below for more details and to register."

You can also post again when the webinar day is approaching and say:

"Just two days left until our webinar on 'Mastering Remote Team Management'! Here's a sneak peek at what we'll be covering. We've tailored our content to address the common challenges many of you shared here, such as communication barriers, project coordination, and maintaining team morale. Don't miss out on discovering key strategies that can transform the way you lead remotely. Find the link for last-minute registrations in the comments!"

By following these steps, you are not just promoting a webinar but are actively engaging with your audience, understanding their needs, and providing a solution.

This approach ensures that your link promotion feels natural and valuable, increasing the likelihood of higher engagement and attendance.

Through strategic, thoughtful link sharing on LinkedIn, you can drive significant traffic to your external content without sacrificing engagement on the platform itself.

When you provide value within your posts and make the link a secondary offer, you create a win-win scenario: your audience gains useful insights directly on LinkedIn, and those interested in diving deeper have the link right there to take them further.

# Chapter Nine

# Leveraging Hashtags for Maximum LinkedIn Reach

Hashtags on LinkedIn are like the spices in a gourmet dish, they can elevate your content and make it more discoverable to the right audience. But just like in cooking, the key is to use them judiciously and effectively.

Have you ever wondered why some posts do well on LinkedIn while others sink unnoticed? The secret often lies in those sharp little tags at the end of posts. When used wisely, they enhance your posts' visibility and ensure that your insights reach those who will value them most.

Let's dive into the world of hashtags and uncover how you can harness their power to amplify your LinkedIn presence.

## Understanding the Role of Hashtags

Think of hashtags as keys that unlock various thematic rooms on LinkedIn where professionals and business owners gather to share and discuss their interests.

By tagging your posts accurately, you invite people into your conversation, expanding your content's reach beyond your immediate connections. This can significantly increase engagement and opportunities for professional and business growth.

### Developing a Hashtag Strategy

Here's are the steps you need to take for effective hashtag usage:

### Select Relevant Hashtags:

Start by identifying the core themes of your post. Use specific and relevant hashtags that directly relate to your content.

For instance, It's tempting to slap on a #leadership or #innovation onto everything, but will that really help your specific post about diversity in tech reach the right viewers? Tailor your hashtags to your content to ensure they are reaching the people who will find it most valuable.

if you're posting about a recent advancement in digital marketing, consider using #DigitalMarketing instead of the more generic #Business.

You can find relevant hashtags by observing what tags influencers in your field are using and by using LinkedIn's search feature to see how many posts are associated with a particular hashtag. This helps in understanding which tags are trending and active.

**Research and Refine:**

Dedicate time to explore hashtags used by your industry peers and competitors. Tools like LinkedIn's hashtag suggestions when creating a post or external tools that analyse hashtag popularity can provide insights into what's currently gaining traction.

Regularly update your hashtag lists because the popularity and relevance of hashtags can change. Keep an eye on industry trends and adapt your hashtags accordingly.

**Mix Popular and Niche Tags:**

Balance your hashtag use between broad-appeal tags that attract a larger audience and niche-specific tags that target a specific group. For example, #Leadership is broad, while #TechLeadership is more specific and likely to attract a focused audience.

Using niche hashtags allows you to engage with a community that is highly interested in your content, which can lead to higher quality interactions.

**Keep It Moderate:**

Limit the number of hashtags you use per post to avoid appearing spammy. LinkedIn suggests using no more than three to five hashtags.

Choose your hashtags strategically; each one should serve a purpose and be directly relevant to the content of your post.

I would also recommend 2 to 3 of your hashtags having at least 10k following to have maximum impact.

Avoid overloading posts with irrelevant hashtags as it can dilute your message and annoy your audience.

**Monitor and Adapt:**

Use LinkedIn's analytics to track how different hashtags perform in terms of reach and engagement. Note which hashtags consistently perform well and integrate them into your strategy.

Be adaptable in your approach by testing new hashtags and phasing out ones that do not perform well. This keeps your content fresh and aligned with current trends.

**Create Branded Hashtags:**

For personal branding or specific campaigns, you can create and use a unique hashtag. This can be a game-changer for building a community or promoting a series of posts.

Each time you use this tag, you're reinforcing your brand or campaign, inviting your audience to follow along through a cohesive narrative thread.

**Examples of Effective Hashtag Use**

**Scenario:** You are sharing insights on inclusive hiring practices.

Hashtags to consider includes #InclusiveHiring, #HRLeaders, #DiversityAndInclusion. These tags are directly relevant and likely followed by professionals interested in HR and workplace diversity.

**Scenario:** You are promoting a webinar on the future of renewable energy.

Hashtags to consider include #RenewableEnergy, #Sustainability, #CleanTech. This combination reaches an audience specifically interested in sustainability and innovations in technology.

**Scenario:** You are writing a post on innovative project management techniques; instead of a broad tag like #Business, use more specific hashtags like #ProjectManagement, #InnovativeLeadership, and #TeamProductivity to draw in professionals interested in these areas.

**Scenario:** if discussing diversity initiatives in tech, go beyond #Diversity to include #TechDiversity, #InclusiveTech, and #WomenInTech. These refine the audience and highlight specific sectors and issues within the broader topic.

Effective hashtag use on LinkedIn is about harmonising your content with the interests of your target audience through strategic tag selection. This approach ensures your posts do more than just appear on the platform—they resonate with and engage the right viewers.

Remember, hashtags are more than just add-ons; they are integral tools that enhance the discoverability and impact of your professional content.

By thoughtfully selecting and employing hashtags, you transform them from mere metadata into powerful allies in your LinkedIn strategy.

# Chapter Ten

# Storytelling Mastery: Captivating Your LinkedIn Audience

Every professional or business owner on LinkedIn wants to be heard despite the challenges of gaining visibility. So, how do you ensure that your voice reaches and resonates deeply with your audience?

The secret weapon is storytelling.

This ancient art transforms your LinkedIn presence by weaving your professional experiences into engaging narratives that engage, inspire, and connect on a deeply human level.

This chapter covers the steps you need to hone your storytelling skills to captivate and resonate with your LinkedIn audience.

## Mastering the Art of LinkedIn Storytelling

On LinkedIn, storytelling does more than share information—it builds connections. It turns your achievements and insights into relatable stories that engage emotions and foster a genuine connection with your audience.

When you effectively tell your story, you transform your LinkedIn space from a mere bulletin board of professional updates into a dynamic stage where your career or business journey unfolds.

### Crafting Compelling Stories for LinkedIn

Tailoring your stories to your audience's needs and desires ensures your message hits home. You need to know who they are, the challenges they face, and what inspires them, then tailor your stories in a way that speaks directly to them.

For example, if your primary audience is young entrepreneurs, share stories about overcoming early career challenges, like navigating startup funding or balancing life and work.

This understanding guides the tone, content, and purpose of your narratives, making them relevant and impactful.

What makes a good story?

### A Clear Message

Every story must have a heartbeat, a central message that pulses through its narrative.

What core idea or lesson do you want to convey? Whether it's overcoming adversity, a moment of unexpected insight, or a milestone achievement, this message should resonate with clarity and power throughout your story.

**A Magnetic Opening**

Grab attention right from the start. Use a hook that intrigues and invites—ask a compelling question, state a provocative fact, or begin with a surprising anecdote.

For instance, "I never thought a coffee spill would lead to my breakthrough career moment, but here's how it happened..."

This is a great way to pique their interest and tease them into wanting to read further.

People are naturally curious, and this element of psychology draws them in.

**Rich Descriptive Details**

Don't just tell your audience what happened. Bring them into the scene. Describe the sights, sounds, and emotions that surrounded your experiences.

Paint with words so your audience can visualise and feel the journey with you.

Example: "Walking into the buzzing startup incubator, I felt a mix of nerves and excitement. Every corner was filled with eager faces, all chasing their big idea."

**Structure Your Story as a Journey**

Good stories have a beginning, middle, and end. Start with the situation or problem, navigate through the actions or challenges faced, and end with the resolution or insights gained.

Example: Start with the challenge of launching a new product, continue through the hurdles of market acceptance, and conclude with the success of achieving your first £1 million in sales.

This flow maintains engagement and mirrors the ups and downs that everyone experiences in their professional or business lives.

**Use Visuals to Complement Your Narrative**

Support your storytelling with relevant images, videos, or infographics that add depth to your narrative and appeal visually to your audience.

For example, you can include a photo from an event you're describing or a chart that illustrates the results of the strategies you're discussing.

When you have an image that makes an impact, you get more eyes on your posts.

**Engage with a Purposeful Conclusion**

Every story should leave the audience with something, a thought, a feeling, a call to action.

Example: "Have you faced similar challenges in your career? Share your story in the comments or message me, I'd love to hear from you!"

Whether you prompt them to share their own experiences, ask a thought-provoking question, or encourage them to reach out for collaboration, your conclusion should clearly signal what you hope to achieve with your narrative.

**The Power of Authenticity in Storytelling**

Authenticity should be the cornerstone of your storytelling approach on LinkedIn. Being genuine in sharing your successes, failures, and lessons learned, you build trust and relatability with your audience.

This connection is what transforms a mere LinkedIn contact into a loyal follower and, potentially, a collaborator or client.

Imagine you are a leadership coach sharing your journey of developing a groundbreaking coaching method.

Your post could detail the initial doubts you had, the breakthrough moment at a major conference, and how you've since transformed the careers of dozens of leaders.

End with an invitation to a free webinar where you delve deeper into this method, providing a direct way for readers to engage with you further.

**Incorporating Diversity and Inclusion in Your Stories**

As you craft your narratives, remember to include diverse perspectives and experiences that reflect the wide array of backgrounds represented in your audience.

This enhances the relatability of your stories and underscores your commitment to inclusivity within your professional or business branding.

I use stories regularly and focus on incorporating diversity and inclusion in my stories. Depending on what I am working on at that time, I use different angles to tell the same story.

When telling your story it is important to avoid stereotypes and tokenism. You should also be aware of cultural sensitivity when sharing to prevent discrimination.

Effective storytelling on LinkedIn elevates your profile by making your professional or business journey accessible and engaging.

It invites your audience to experience your evolving story of challenges, triumphs, and growth. Through your stories, you offer more than insight; you offer inspiration and a path for others to follow.

# Chapter Eleven

# Mastering LinkedIn's Artful Language for Success

Words are the lifeblood of effective communication on LinkedIn. They have the power to persuade, engage, and inspire action. Everyone seems to be shouting, yet only a few voices capture the crowd's attention. How do they do it? The secret lies in mastering the art of LinkedIn copywriting.

In this chapter, we'll cover the tips and tricks you need to use to write persuasive copy that appeals to a diverse audience. Your copy also needs to speak to your target audience, turning passive readers into active participants and supporters of your professional journey or business.

## Crafting Copy that Converts

Your ability to craft compelling copy can set you apart, turning your profile, posts, and messages into magnets that attract the right kind of attention.

Your copy all starts with a good understanding of who you are talking to, their challenges, needs, and goals. Tailoring your message to address these points increases your relevance and the impact of your copy.

Always start by asking, "What's in it for them?"

Your copy should always be about them and not about you.

Here are the steps to take for creating and effective LinkedIn copy:

**Be Clear and Concise:**

LinkedIn is a professional platform where clarity and brevity are valued. Plus the attention span of people has reduced drastically.

Use punchy, direct sentences that make your point without meandering. Get to the heart of the message quickly—your audience will appreciate it.

Use straightforward language and avoid industry jargon unless it's commonly understood by your audience. Keep your messages brief but impactful.

For example, instead of saying, "We're leveraging our core competencies to synergise outcomes," say, "We're using our key skills to improve results."

**Use Active Voice:**

Write with an active voice to create dynamic and engaging content. For example, "I led a team that increased sales by 20% last quarter" is more powerful than "A team was led by me, which increased sales by 20% last quarter." This shift tightens your writing and also injects energy into your narrative.

Active voice makes your writing stronger and more direct. It clearly assigns action, making your sentences livelier and more engaging.

**Employ Storytelling Techniques:**

Even in short copy, storytelling can be powerful. Share brief narratives that illustrate your points or highlight your experiences.

These stories should be relatable and align with the interests of your audience, making your copy more engaging and memorable. Stories also help humanise your content and makes abstract concepts real.

For example: "When I first joined the team, our project was struggling. By refocusing our strategy, we turned a failing project into a major win, enhancing our department's reputation."

**Incorporate Strategic Keywords and Hashtags:**

Use keywords that are relevant to your industry and role to improve the visibility of your posts. However, balance is key—overstuffing can make your copy feel forced and unauthentic.

Similarly, include relevant hashtags to extend your reach but keep them focused and related to the topic.

For example, you can say: "Join our #WebinarWednesday to explore the latest trends in #DigitalMarketing and learn how to boost your #SEO strategy."

This will make your content discoverable to a wider audience on the platform through search results.

**Highlight Benefits, Not Just Features:**

When discussing your services, products, or initiatives, emphasise how they benefit the reader. Instead of just listing features, explain how these features solve problems or improve professional lives.

Instead of "Our software has the latest encryption technology," you could say, "Our software secures your data against breaches, protecting your company's valuable information."

**Call to Action:**

Always include a clear and specific call to action at the end of your copy. What do you want your audience to do after reading your post? Whether it's visiting a website, joining a conversation, or checking out a service, your call to action should be direct and easy to follow.

For example: "Click here to register for our free webinar and start transforming your strategy today!"

**Integrating Diverse and Inclusive Language in Your Copy:**

When crafting your LinkedIn copy, it's crucial to use language that is inclusive and reflects a diverse professional community.

Avoid jargon that might alienate parts of your audience and use examples or metaphors that are universally relatable. This not only broadens your appeal but also demonstrates your commitment to creating an inclusive professional environment.

Inclusive language is a form of communication that recognises and respects the diversity of individuals.

It is important to use inclusive language in your copy to create a cohesive and respectful environment. When communicating with clients and customers, there are specific words or phrases to avoid.

For example, instead of referring to someone as "handicapped", you could say " Disabled Person" or if it is their preference, use a person centred approach "person with disability".

Here are more examples of words you can use:

- 'Pregnant woman' or 'Pregnant person'
- Instead of 'BAME/BME' say 'Black person' or ' Asian Person'
- Instead of "Chairman/Chairperson" use "Chair, Facilitator"
- Instead of "Salesman/Saleswoman" use "Salesperson, Representative:
- Instead of "Stewardess" use "Flight Attendant"

- Instead of "Male/Female" use "Person, Individual"
- Instead of "Negro/Colored" use "Black, African American"
- Instead of "Homosexual" use "Gay, Lesbian"
- Instead of "Old people" use "Elderly, Seniors"

There are a number of sources that can contribute to a business owner using non-inclusive language, even if they do not intend to do so.

One common source is a lack of awareness or understanding of the impact that language can have on different groups of people.

This can be due to a lack of exposure to diverse perspectives or experiences, or a lack of education or training on inclusive language practices.

Another source of non-inclusive language can be cultural or societal norms and biases, which may have been learned and internalised over time.

Sometimes, you may use non-inclusive language without realising the harm it can cause simply because it has been accepted and used widely. But when you make that conscious effort, especially within your copy, it indicates your commitment to the cause.

Crafting impactful LinkedIn copy requires a blend of clarity, strategy, and empathy. Your focus should be on what your audience cares about and how you can add value to their lives.

You can transform your copy from mere text into a compelling narrative that invites engagement and builds connections. Remember, every word you write is an opportunity to resonate more deeply with your community.

Would you like to take my Diversity and inclusion audit to deepen your awareness?

Scan the below QR code to take my 3 minutes personalised audit.

## Chapter Twelve

# Post Precision: Unlocking the Science Behind LinkedIn's Top Hits

With lots of posts being published daily on LinkedIn, you need to be able to craft posts that can compete in the spotlight. How do you ensure your content not only captures attention but also maintains it?

To achieve this, you need to understand the science behind what makes a LinkedIn post a top hit. In this chapter, we'll cover how to create posts that have the potential to become top hits and the science behind it.

## Precision in Post Creation

Crafting standout LinkedIn posts requires a blend of engaging content, strategic timing, and keen audience awareness. When you analyse patterns in top-performing posts, you can unlock powerful insights that elevate your content strategy from guesswork to precision.

The preceding chapters have covered all that needs to be done, and to make this work, you need to put together all the lessons, tips and tricks. Some require just subtle changes to the way you write, while others need a total revamp of your writing style.

## Elements of A Viral LinkedIn Post

Let's take a look at some of the elements that can make a LinkedIn post go viral:

### The Headline

The foundation of any viral LinkedIn post is a striking headline. Think of your headline as the front door to your post; it needs to be inviting enough to draw people in.

A great headline sparks curiosity or promises valuable insights in a way that feels almost irresistible. You might think a straightforward headline is enough, but have you considered the power of invoking a question or a bold statement that challenges conventional wisdom?

You can share a story or offer a shocking stat or myth to boost your headline.

Imagine you're a career coach, and instead of a generic headline like "Career Tips," you opt for "Why 90% of CVs Get Thrown Out." Immediately, you've piqued interest with a bold statement that promises insider knowledge.

This headline hooks readers because it challenges common assumptions and promises a revelation.

Once they've entered through that captivating headline, readers need a relatable narrative to keep them engaged. Stories resonate deeply; they make your professional insights personal and universal all at once.

Why not share a turning point in your career or a lesson that came the hard way? It's not just what you tell, but how you make your audience feel, drawing them into the ups and downs of your professional journey or business.

**Relatable Narrative**

But a narrative alone won't cut it unless it provides practical value. LinkedIn users are on the hunt for tips, strategies, and insights they can apply instantly in their own lives.

Maybe you have industry-specific advice or a productivity hack you swear by. Offering clear, actionable steps that solve common problems can transform your post from interesting to indispensable.

As a career coach for women, I often share stories about the daily struggles and triumphs of being a career mum of six under six.

I also cover success stories associated with my clients and these are everyday challenges that women can relate with.

**Practical Value**

Creating posts that are value-packed makes it appealing to your target audience. If the post addresses a pain point in a particular niche and outlines a solution that users can take and implement right away, then it stands a higher chance of going viral.

Imagine if John, an SEO expert, wrote a post titled "Five SEO Mistakes That Could Tank Your Website" and outlined common pitfalls along with easy-to-implement solutions.

He then makes each tip actionable and directly applicable. This will turn his post into a mini-masterclass that his audience could use immediately, enhancing its shareability.

Another example is a short checklist that gives actionable steps. For example

Checklist for creating a valuable post:

1. Hook [ ]
2. Storytelling [ ]
3. Value [ ]
4. Spark conversation [ ]
5. Hashtag [ ]

This can be placed in an image format to encourage sharing.

**Strong Visuals**

Don't forget the role of strong visuals. In a sea of text, an image or a video can act as an island of relief. Whether it's a striking infographic that breaks down complex data or a heartfelt video message, visuals can significantly amplify your post's appeal and retention.

Consider a post with a captivating infographic that illustrates the rising trends in diversity and inclusion among small businesses.

The visual alone draws the eye, but its data provides value, making such a post likely to be saved and shared.

Visuals often act as the gateway to deeper engagement with content.

**Engagement Hooks**

Engagement doesn't end when the story does, which is where a clever engagement hook comes into play.

Pose a question, invite feedback, or suggest a follow-up action at the end of your post.

You need to practicalize this to boost your metrics and at the same time, spark genuine conversation and build community around your content.

This subtle element can stimulate comments or discussions and make your followers feel like part of a community conversation. Everyone loves the feeling of being heard and being given a chance to express their feelings.

**Timeliness and Relevance**

The timing of your post also plays a crucial role. Timeliness and relevance are your allies. Connecting your content to current events or trending topics can give it an extra boost of relevancy that prompts shares and discussions.

Have you considered linking your expertise to ongoing industry developments or news events? Or perhaps talking about a day being celebrated as it relates to your niche and sharing an inspiring story around it. You can then segue and add a call to action leading to an offer or resource for impact.

As a diversity and inclusion coach I keep track of the Diversity calendar full of events that I can talk about and share with my audience.

Depending on your niche, you can always find relevant events to add to your post.

**Authenticity**

Another element that might surprise you is the power of authenticity. Let your true self shine through your content. People gravitate towards honesty and can sniff out insincerity from a mile away.

Could it be that simply being yourself could be your strongest asset on LinkedIn? The answer is absolutely "Yes", and I use this all the time.

Sharing stories of my past experiences, from motherhood challenges to career and business growth and everything in between, makes me appear real and authentic to my audience.

Although these stories reveal my vulnerability, they struck a chord with many, leading to a flood of supportive comments and shares.

Authenticity like this builds trust and fosters genuine connections.

**Simplicity**

There's also the power of simplicity. Have you noticed how posts that distil complex concepts into simple, understandable language tend to do well? Clear, jargon-free communication makes your content accessible to a broader audience, enhancing its shareability.

No one wants to rack their brain just because they want to read your post. They would just move on.

**Conversational Tone**

A post that reads like a conversation rather than a formal announcement invites more comments and interactions. This approach makes your content feel less like a lecture and more like a dialogue, inviting interaction and fostering a friendly atmosphere.

Why not try addressing your readers directly as you would in a face-to-face conversation? This strategy not only makes your content more relatable but also encourages your followers to participate in the discussion.

For instance, instead of simply stating facts or opinions, frame them as questions or prompts for feedback.

You could say:

- "What's your take on the latest market trends?"

- "I'm genuinely curious—what are your thoughts on the hybrid work model?" or
- "I'd love to hear how others are adapting to remote work. Share your stories below!"

This approach breaks down barriers and cultivates a community vibe where everyone feels welcome to contribute their thoughts and experiences.

**Relevant Hashtags and Keywords**

Effectively using keywords and hashtags can dramatically increase the visibility of your posts to a wider audience. Keywords make your content searchable and thus more likely to be discovered by LinkedIn users interested in specific topics.

Hashtags serve a similar function but also link your posts to larger, ongoing conversations on the platform.

When incorporating keywords and hashtags, be strategic. Choose keywords that are relevant to the content and resonate with your industry.

For hashtags, use a combination of broad and niche tags to balance reach and relevance.

For example, if you're posting about leadership development, you might include hashtags like #Leadership, #CareerGrowth, and #ProfessionalDevelopment. Remember, overusing hashtags can appear spammy, so keep it to a reasonable number—typically no more than five.

**Universal Appeal**

Inclusion is key, and a viral post often has an element of universal appeal. It speaks to a common experience or challenge, making it relevant to a diverse audience. How wide can the net of your story reach?

For example, a post titled "The Things We Wish We Knew at Our First Job", which includes short anecdotes from several professionals across different industries, will naturally appeal to many. After all, a lot of professionals have had their share of experience in their first jobs.

This universal theme tapped into a shared experience and will encourage a wide range of professionals to reflect and engage with the post.

**Call To Action**

Lastly, the most shared posts often include a call to action. This could be as simple as asking your readers to share their experiences, or it could involve directing them to a link for more information. What step are you encouraging your readers to take after engaging with your post?

You must have this well thought out such that your story aligns and amplifies your content urging your readers to take the right action.

When you put these elements together—each adding its unique flavour to the mix—you can craft LinkedIn posts with high visibility and engagement.

One last thing to note is to opt for the Premium LinkedIn package and enjoy maximum visibility as LinkedIn favours the posts of its paying members.

## Top Hit Stories: Crafting Viral Success

Achieving viral success on LinkedIn can significantly amplify your professional brand and expand your influence across a global network. We'll analyse LinkedIn posts that have used the right strategy and went viral. Through their stories, we'll uncover the tactics and insights that can help you craft your viral hit.

**My Viral Story**

Let's start with a personal revelation that challenged a common myth and connected deeply with many on LinkedIn.

I shared an intimate glimpse into my life, discussing the challenges and triumphs of being a mother to five children under the age of seven while running a successful business and managing dyslexia.

This post resonated widely, garnering 138,768 impressions and 68 comments, proving that personal, authentic content can indeed lead to wide engagement.

Here's a snippet

The result I got definitely felt good.

The truth is you do not need to have a million likes to feel like a star on LinkedIn. The logic is to keep building and improving.

Let's also take a look at five examples of viral success posts on LinkedIn, as analysed by Paul Petrone.

#1: Amy Volas- The Art of Keeping Your Best Sellers

Amy's post delved deep into the unspoken truths of sales, providing a long, detailed narrative that captured the real essence of a sales professional's world. Despite its length, the post was punchy and engaging, making readers nod in agreement and share widely.

Key takeaways:

- **Length Can Work:** Long posts can perform exceptionally well if they're engaging and offer new insights.

- **Speak Unspoken Truths:** Addressing commonly felt but rarely discussed feelings or challenges can resonate deeply.
- **Keep It Fun:** Even serious topics benefit from a lively, engaging tone.

#2: Mark Kosoglow- Winning the Impossible Deals

Mark's post shared a counter-intuitive strategy about focusing on winning tough deals rather than the easy picks.

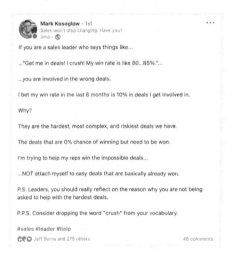

His insights were:

- **Eye-Catching Openings**: Start with a strong, attention-grabbing statement.
- **Share Personal Experiences**: Authentic stories from personal experience enhance credibility and engagement.
- **Challenge Common Beliefs**: Posts that offer new perspectives or challenge the status quo tend to stand out.

#3: Gabrielle 'GB' Blackwell - Practical Management Advice

GB's advice on management was straightforward, actionable, and cut through the noise with its clarity.

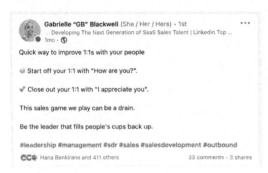

Takeaways include:

- **Actionability:** Offering clear, executable steps can significantly increase a post's usefulness and shareability.
- **Accessibility:** Ensuring content is easy to understand and quick to read can broaden its reach.
- **Real Talk:** Authenticity in content, especially about the challenges of work life, enhances relatability.

#### #4: Anthony Natoli - Six Tips for Stellar Prospecting

Anthony's post was a treasure trove of actionable tips for prospecting, structured almost like a mini-guide or template.

Key insights:

- **High Value:** Ensure content is packed with practical, actionable guidance.
- **Strong Stance:** Don't be afraid to be bold in your assertions, as long as you can back them up with solid advice.
- **Template Format:** Providing a clear, usable format can help others implement your advice easily.

#5: Amber Naslund - Challenging Workplace Norms

Amber's post addressed a poignant, relatable issue about gender norms in professional settings, delivered with boldness and precision.

Why it worked:

- **Relatable Pain Points:** Tapping into widespread but under-discussed issues can spark widespread identification and sharing.
- **Bold and Direct:** Confidence in expression can make your content powerful and memorable.
- **Seek Change:** Posts that not only discuss problems but also call for action inspire engagement and discussion.

These stories not only inspire but also teach us that there isn't a one-size-fits-all approach to viral success.

Whether sharing deeply personal stories, providing valuable insights, or challenging existing norms, the key lies in knowing your audience well and presenting content that strikes a chord.

Remember, the goal isn't just to go viral; it's to create content that moves, influences, and connects.

## Summary

Each chapter in this book has been designed to transform your LinkedIn approach from passive to strategic. Here's a quick tour of what we've learned, accompanied by a handy to-do list to keep you on track:

**Unveiling Your Niche**

Defining your niche and who you want to connect with is key to succeeding on LinkedIn.

**To do:**

- Explore the evolution and unique features of LinkedIn
- Identify and understand your personal or professional niche
- Research your customer avatar
- Study examples and case studies of niche transformations
- Apply insights to establish your unique presence on LinkedIn

**Setting the Stage**

Here, we covered the foundational aspects of creating a standout LinkedIn profile. This isn't just about having a professional photo or a snappy headline (though they help), it's about crafting a profile that speaks volumes about you.

**To-Do:**

- Update your profile picture and background photo
- Refine your headline to capture your essence in a few words
- Craft a compelling summary that tells your story
- Optimise your profile for SEO with relevant keywords
- List skills that are current and in demand in your industry
- Request recommendations and endorsements from colleagues
- Update headline , banner, etc.) for inclusivity
- Craft a compelling About section that emphasises diversity
- Feature skills, endorsements

- Add volunteer experiences that reflect inclusive values

**Building Your Network**

This chapter focused on strategic network expansion—connecting not just widely, but wisely. It's not about the size of your network, but the strength of your connections.

**To-Do:**

- Identify industry leaders and potential mentors to connect with.
- Join LinkedIn groups in your field.
- Engage with posts by liking, commenting, and sharing.
- Send personalised connection requests.
- Follow companies you're interested in working with or for.
- Regularly update your network with your professional developments.

**Create Engaging Content**

We dove into the art of creating content that not only catches the eye but also holds attention. Quality trumps quantity every time.

**To-Do:**

- Plan your content calendar for consistent posting.
- Create posts that provide value, such as tips or industry insights.
- Use rich media like images and videos to enhance engagement.
- Write articles to establish thought leadership.
- Ask questions in your posts to encourage interaction.
- Share updates and news relevant to your industry.
- Monitor which types of content receive the most engagement and adjust accordingly.

**Inclusivity Wins**

Inclusivity isn't just right; it's smart. Posts that resonate across diverse groups tend to see more engagement and reach.

**To-Do:**

- Use inclusive language in your content.
- Highlight diverse voices and perspectives in your posts.
- Share content that addresses universal challenges in your field.
- Engage with and support content from diverse networks.
- Include captions and descriptive text to make your content accessible.
- Educate yourself on cultural competencies.
- Review your content's performance in different demographic groups.

**Analysing to Optimise**

Data might seem daunting until you realise it tells you exactly what your audience loves. Here, we learned to interpret engagement metrics as a roadmap for content strategy.

**To-Do:**

- Regularly check your LinkedIn analytics.
- Set specific metrics goals for each post type.
- Experiment with posting at different times and days to see what works best.
- Keep track of which content formats perform best.
- Note the demographics of your most engaged viewers.
- Adjust your content strategy based on analytics insights.
- Use A/B testing for your posts to refine your approach.

**Leveraging LinkedIn Features**

This chapter explored the various LinkedIn features that can amplify your visibility and engagement. It's about using the platform's tools to their fullest potential, from LinkedIn Stories to Polls and beyond.

**To-Do:**

- Experiment with LinkedIn Stories to share day-to-day professional updates.
- Use Polls to gather opinions and engage your network.
- Explore LinkedIn Live for real-time engagement.

- Utilise LinkedIn's newsletter feature to regularly connect with your followers.
- Take advantage of the Featured section to highlight your key achievements.
- Create and join LinkedIn Events to network and share knowledge.
- Regularly update your skills and endorsements to keep your profile current.

**Personal Branding on LinkedIn**

Here we focused on crafting a personal brand that resonates and remains memorable across your network. Your brand isn't just what you do; it's the story of who you are.

**To-Do:**

- Define your unique value proposition clearly.
- Consistently communicate your brand across all posts and interactions.
- Share stories and experiences that illustrate your brand's principles.
- Engage with other brands and professionals that align with your values.
- Regularly review and refine your brand as your career evolves.
- Use a professional tone that reflects your brand's voice.
- Monitor and manage your online reputation actively.

**Networking Strategies**

Effective networking isn't about collecting contacts—it's about cultivating relationships that are mutually beneficial. This chapter provided tactics for turning connections into meaningful professional relationships.

**To-Do:**

- Reach out to new connections with a personalised note.
- Schedule virtual coffee meetings to deepen relationships.
- Offer value through sharing relevant information or assistance.
- Regularly engage with your connections' content.
- Create and participate in LinkedIn group discussions.
- Introduce connections to each other to facilitate networking.

- Keep a record of key information about your connections to personalise interactions.

## Mastering LinkedIn's Artful Language for Success

We delve into the art of LinkedIn copywriting, which is the backbone of effective communication on the platform. Here, you learn to craft persuasive copy that not only speaks to your target audience but transforms passive readers into active participants. It starts with understanding who you're addressing—know their challenges, needs, and goals. Your copy should always focus on the reader with a clear answer to "What's in it for them?"

**To-Do:**

- Use catchy hooks to create the element of curiosity
- Write punchy, direct sentences and get to the point quickly to keep your audience engaged.
- Energise your content by stating actions clearly and directly, making your points more compelling.
- Incorporate brief, relatable stories that highlight your experiences and resonate with your audience.
- Smartly use relevant keywords and hashtags to increase the visibility and reach of your posts.
- Always emphasise how your services or insights benefit the reader, solving problems or enhancing their professional life.
- End your posts with a clear, actionable step you want your audience to take next.
- Ensure your language respects and acknowledges diverse backgrounds, making your content universally relatable and respectful.
- Add compelling call to actions

## Viral Post Precision

Here we explore the elements that make LinkedIn posts go viral, from engaging headlines to visuals that break up text and draw the eye.

**To-Do:**

- Use headlines that invoke questions or bold statements to spark curiosity and draw readers in.
- Share personal stories or experiences that underscore your points and make your content resonate on a personal level.

- Provide clear, actionable advice or tips that your audience can apply immediately.
- Use images, videos, or infographics to enhance your message and engage visually.
- Conclude posts with questions or prompts that encourage reader interaction and discussion.
- Leverage timing and relevance by linking your content to current events or trending topics for added visibility.
- Be Authentic and Simple: Maintain authenticity and simplicity to ensure your content is genuine and easily digestible.

## Bonus

Now that you're all caught up, how about we map out where you're headed? This isn't just about following steps; it's about charting a course that feels right for you. Ready to get your hands dirty?

### Roadmap to Follow

- **Set Clear Goals.** What's your beacon in the fog? Sales leads, job offers, industry influence? Nail that down first.
- **Targeted Inclusive Content Creation.** Who are you talking to? What do they need to hear? Tailor your message like you're crafting a key that fits right into the lock of opportunity.
- **Engage, Then Engage Some More.** Ever thrown a hello into the void and heard nothing back? Let's make sure that doesn't happen on LinkedIn. Comment, share, respond—make some noise.
- **Rinse and Repeat.** Got a post that did well? Why? Can you do it again? Don't reinvent the wheel every time; sometimes, a little tweak is all you need.

### Crafting a Strategic Content Plan

Let's weave everything together into a master plan.

**Content Creation:** Start with stories, not statements. Need to share a professional win? Frame it as a journey with highs and lows, inviting your audience to walk it with you. This isn't just sharing; it's storytelling.

**Content Scheduling:** Timing isn't just a thing—it's everything. That killer post might not stand a chance if it goes live when everyone's asleep or worse, when they're drowning in other content. Think about when your audience checks their feed. First thing in the morning? During their lunch break?

**Content Analysis:** This is where you turn detective. Which posts got hearts racing? Which ones flopped? Data will tell you, and once you know, you can double down on what works. Surprising, right? Sometimes, less is more if it's the right less.

**Goal Setting:** This is your north star. Without it, how will you know if you've arrived? Set goals that challenge you but are as clear as day. Want 500 new followers? Aim for it. Looking for speaking opportunities? Go get them.

**Feedback Incorporation:** Ever thought you nailed it but your audience yawned? Or that quick post you almost didn't publish got tons of love? Feedback is your goldmine. Dig into comments, messages, likes. Adjust, adapt, and improve.

Creating a content plan that leads to triumph on LinkedIn isn't about following a secret formula; it's about knowing your tools, understanding your audience, and crafting inclusive messages that not only speak to them but also speak for you.

Grab all my Profitable and Inclusive LinkedIn book resources by scanning the QR code below:

https://samanthalubanzu.kartra.com/page/LinkedIn-Book-Resources

Want to transform your LinkedIn profile into a powerful lead-generation machine?

Are you ready to attract your ideal diverse opportunities?

To continue your journey and Unlock the Power of LinkedIn, join my **Profitable and Inclusive Linkedin Mastery Pro: Leveraging The LinkedIn Platform To Accelerate Into New Income Brackets While Being Diverse and Inclusive.**

**The 8-Week Course**

Profitable & Inclusive LinkedIn Pro is an intensive 8-week course designed to help you:

- Develop a data-driven LinkedIn strategy that attracts high-quality leads
- Craft targeted content that engages your ideal audience.
- Convert connections into paying clients and boost your bottom line.

All whilst being inclusive, making you highly attractive for diverse audiences and corporates too!

Find out more by scanning the above QR code.

Or you can join my Career Accelerator Programme.

www.samanthalubanzu.com

Find out more by scanning the above QR code.

Where you'll learn:

- Module 1: **Self-Awakening**
- Module 2: **Your Strength Finder**
- Module 3: **The Market Research Alignment Plan**
- Module 4: **Develop your Winning Career Strategy**
- Module 5: **Inspire to Influence**
- Module 6: **Personal Brand Accelerator**

**Testimonial:**

"Samantha was able to support and coach me in preparation for my next career step. She motivated me and steered me in the right direction as well as filling me with confidence when I went for the interview (which I was successful) Samantha is truly inspirational and has played a pivotal role in my career development."

**-Uche Erhuero (HR Professional)**

Want to grab my FREE LinkedIn 30-Day Challenge for content ideas?

Send an email to Samantha@samanthalubanzu.com with the subject "30-day challenge"